Tiwalola Adebayo (née Ogunlesi) is a globally recognized and qualified life coach, TEDx Speaker, positive psychology specialist, author, podcast host and founder of Confident and Killing It. And if there is one thing Tiwa gets, it's how to unlock your most confident self.

Having struggled with low self-esteem throughout her teenage years, Tiwa founded Confident and Killing It in 2017 to help girls and women overcome the very issues she faced. She is passionate about breaking generational cycles of low self-esteem and championing change, both practically and proactively.

Filled with energy, enthusiasm and charisma, Tiwa uses positive and powerful tools to empower others to trust themselves, speak up and take action in life.

@tiwalowla
www.confidentandkillingit.com

Also by Tiwalola Adebayo

Confident and Killing It: A practical guide to overcoming fear and unlocking your most empowered self

Confident *and* Killing it

A Toolkit for Life

TIWALOLA ADEBAYO

HQ

ONE PLACE. MANY STORIES

HQ
An imprint of HarperCollins*Publishers* Ltd
1 London Bridge Street
London SE1 9GF

www.harpercollins.co.uk

HarperCollins*Publishers*
Macken House, 39/40 Mayor Street Upper,
Dublin 1, D01 C9W8, Ireland

This edition 2026
1
First published in Great Britain by HQ,
an imprint of HarperCollins*Publishers* Ltd 2026

 A catalogue record for this book is available from the British Library.

ISBN: 9780008518226

This book is set in 10.7/15.5 pt. Minion by Type-it AS, Norway

Printed and bound in the UK using 100% Renewable Electricity by CPI Group (UK) Ltd

FSC www.fsc.org
MIX
Paper | Supporting responsible forestry
FSC® C013604

To the women who showed me what it truly means to be unstoppable: my mother, Adenike Ogunlesi, and grandmothers, Elizabeth-White Okuboyejo and Rufina Durogbola Ogunlesi.

And to you, for loving yourself enough to start this journey.

CONTENTS

INTRODUCTION

Have you ever wondered what it would feel like to have unshakeable self-belief? To be able to say, 'This is what I want to do,' and have everything within you conspire to make it happen? That's confidence. It's the belief that you are capable of succeeding in whatever you want to do in life and becoming whoever you want to be. As well as a belief, it's a practice. And the best part? Anyone can build this skill with knowledge and intentionality.

Confidence is a never-ending journey. It's a journey that is bumpy at times, but it's the most enlightening, rewarding and life-changing journey you'll ever embark on. Trust me, I've been on it for years now.

Most people think I'm a confidence coach because I've just been confident my whole life, but it's actually the exact opposite: I'm a confidence coach because I know exactly what it feels like to have a Mean Girl in your mind, judging everything you do. I know what it's like to look in the mirror and hate what you see. I know what it's like to live in fear of what others might think. For the longest time, I fought to prove to myself and the people around me that I had something to offer. I was an over-achiever and a people-pleaser. I strived to be seen as the 'good girl' because I thought, 'There's nothing special about me, so as long as I do what I'm told, play by the rules and make people happy, I'll be accepted.'

I was wrong.

My 'wake-up' moment happened when I was 21 – faith and science collided to send me an important message:

I matter simply because I exist.

It was a mindset shift that would change the trajectory of my life forever. I began to realize that I am and will always be good enough, because when God created me, He said I was wonderfully made. I learned that growth doesn't come with age; it requires intentionality and a game plan. And finally, understanding the power of my mind and how I could use it to create the life I desire meant that I became the master of my own fate.

So, what is Confident and Killing It? It's a movement, it's an energy, a mindset, a way of life. It's waking people up to their worth, so they can be confident, unstoppable and dare to live the life they truly desire.

And the honest truth is we need this now more than ever. The UK's first Confidence Index, carried out by Arden University in 2024,[1] showed that only one in ten adults feels highly self-confident. This is a crisis that not enough people are talking about. The study highlighted three core reasons for a lack of self-confidence: a harsh inner critic, a sense of falling behind in career success, and a difficult childhood.

These are the very issues we'll tackle in this book. When asked what would boost their confidence, most people said improving

1 'UK's First Confidence Index', Arden University (8 April 2025). https://arden.ac.uk/knowledge-base/arden-research/uks-first-confidence-index

their appearance or making more money. And while a new outfit or payday can give you a temporary lift, those fixes are surface-level. True confidence is an inside job.

I learned this first-hand. Back in 2016, I was volunteering as a youth leader and saw just how crushingly low the confidence levels were in the girls I mentored. What struck me most was how the core of their insecurities mirrored the very same things my mother, my aunties, and I criticized in ourselves. That's when it hit me: confidence doesn't automatically come with age, money or success. If the root causes aren't addressed, insecure teenage girls grow up to become insecure women – and insecure women raise insecure daughters. And so, the generational cycle of low self-esteem continues.

Starting my own confidence journey completely transformed my life. It felt too good to keep to myself, so I made it my mission to make confidence practical and accessible, because everyone deserves to love and believe in themselves. I didn't begin with a huge following, industry connections or expert credentials. I was just a girl with a voice, a phone, and a story to share. What started as 'cringey' Instagram videos became a global community, a podcast, corporate workshops, an academy – and now this book.

Since the first edition of this book, people have told me that the message of *Confident and Killing It* has changed their lives. It has helped to heal mental health issues, fix broken relationships, and given mothers tools to raise daughters. Teachers have used it to inspire students. People have quit their jobs, started businesses, asked for promotions, started their own communities, left abusive relationships, unlocked the power of their voice – and so much more. Thousands of lives changed because one person had the confidence to bet on herself. Imagine what your story could be by the time you finish this book. You are the answer to someone's prayer. It's time to unlock your most confident self.

If you've picked up this book, it means you're ready to prioritize your growth and well-being. It means you're ready to be brave and confront your limitations.

As you'll come to see, 'Killing It' isn't about traditional views of success. It isn't about money, fame, power, looking like you have it all together, or overworking yourself for progress 'at any cost'. 'Killing It' is about defining success on your own terms. It's about knowing you are a co-creator of your life and playing your part to make sure you're living in alignment with your purpose, strengths, passions and values. It's about creating a life that you're proud of – a life at your own pace that works for you.

Grounded in the science of positive psychology, this book is your personal toolkit, packed with practical, proven confidence-building tips, strategies and insightful mantras that will transform you from the inside out. The advice and frameworks have been tried and tested, taking the guesswork out of personal growth so you can finally overcome limitations like fear, self-doubt, perfectionism and imposter syndrome.

And because transformation goes deeper when you put things into practice, you'll also find a QR code at the back of the book linked to an interactive digital workbook to guide your reflections, along with an online course where I break down key concepts step by step. Whether you prefer to write things down or watch me coach you through them, you'll have the tools to turn ideas into action.

IMPOSTER SYNDROME
Imposter syndrome is a psychological phenomenon where you believe you're an inadequate and incompetent person, despite evidence that indicates you're skilled and successful. You often live in fear of getting 'found out' as a fraud or failure because deep down, you don't feel worthy of your accomplishments and opportunities.

If you've picked up this book, it means you're ready to prioritize your growth and well-being. It means you're ready to be brave and confront your limitations. What it doesn't mean is that you're broken and need fixing. A lot of us go to personal development to fix ourselves. We think we're broken, and so we look to motivational speakers to give us the validation we're so desperately looking for. The truth is you're not broken, you are naturally creative, resourceful and whole. This book is not here to 'fix' you – it's here to wake you up to the greatness that is already within you.

Here's my number one #CAKIMantra:

You matter simply because you exist.

#CAKIMANTRA

You'll come across more of these gems as you read through this book. Feel free to write them out, put them on sticky notes, post them online or make them your screensaver. They're here to remind you of what it means to be Confident and Killing It.

***

While you have everything you need within you, the world doesn't make it easy to show up as your authentic self and in your true power. There are so many societal barriers and systemic issues that make it hard to be a confident woman. But just because it's hard doesn't mean it's impossible.

There is hope.

We can start with working on the things we have control over. Things like internalizing rejection, pursuing perfectionism and fearing failure are self-inflicted confidence killers. We can make a choice not to give them power. The focus of this book is self-mastery, which involves knowing and growing yourself.

I admit there are some things beyond our control, but are we going to sit around and wait for the world to just magically be a better place before we build confidence? No. As an adult, your confidence, like many other things, is your responsibility.

I also want to highlight that things like imposter syndrome and low self-esteem aren't only women's issues. Men doubt themselves too. They aren't superhuman.

But women, more often than men, tend to feel fear and retreat, overthink situations and then never take action. Sound familiar? The more we hesitate, trying to avoid failure by waiting for the perfect moment to act, the fewer opportunities we have to build our confidence, and when we don't build our confidence, we are more likely to hesitate. It's a vicious cycle.

The good news is that no matter who you are or what personality you have, confidence is something you can nurture and express in your own style. I will give you the frameworks and tools to build a solid foundation. The rest is up to you.

Traditional psychology has studied human pain and suffering in the hope that, by learning how to manage these situations, we can alleviate them and be happy. However, positive psychology takes things one step further and looks at the science and intentionality behind boosting our well-being so we can live a full and rich life. The PERMA model, created by the father of positive psychology, Dr Martin Seligman, presents five pillars of well-being that have been scientifically proven to help us manage our emotions, feel passionate about our work, develop meaningful relationships, live out our purpose and celebrate our accomplishments.

PERMA

PERMA stands for:

P – Positive Emotions

E – Engagement

R – Relationships

M – Meaning

A – Accomplishments

I'll be introducing the five pillars to you in more detail throughout the book, alongside simple, practical ways to apply them to your life.

Self-belief and confidence in your abilities should be your norm rather than something that happens on occasion. If it feels out of reach, it's not because you're not capable or it's too late for you now. It's simply because you haven't gotten the right strategy yet. And that's what this book is here to give you: proven tips, tools and strategies so you can take the guesswork out of growth and unlock your next level. Ready to lock in?

1

DISCOVERING YOUR AUTHENTIC SELF

Confidence starts from sitting with yourself in the present moment and exploring what's there – both your strengths and your limitations. You cannot improve on or heal from what you do not acknowledge, so the first step in building confidence is to become self-aware. You must *know* yourself before you can *believe in* yourself.

In this chapter, I'm going to guide you from a fixed mindset to a growth mindset. This journey will help you wake up to your true, authentic self. Authenticity is about being brave enough to be yourself and genuine enough to live according to your values. What you say and what you do must be in sync with what you truly believe.

Here are some fixed mindset traits. If you feel you resonate with any of these, then welcome to the party, you're in the right place and you are not alone.

Authenticity is about being brave enough to be yourself and genuine enough to live according to your values.

A FIXED MINDSET

Leads to a desire to look smart and a tendency to:

- Avoid challenges and always want life to go very smoothly.
- Give up easily in the face of obstacles.
- See effort as pointless and prefer immediate gratification.
- See no value in expressing emotions freely and clearly.
- Want to be loved by everyone and not be open to learning from mistakes.
- Feel threatened by or jealous of the success of others.
- Have a scarcity mindset and believe there's only room for one person to win.

This was me. I ticked every single one of these boxes. On the surface, it looked as though I was winning. I was the good girl who did well in school, I always followed the rules so that people would love me, and I did everything in my power to look as though I had it all together. But behind closed doors, if things didn't go as planned, I would fall apart. Essentially, I was far from being my authentic self.

If this is you right now, please don't stress. This is actually a very exciting opportunity to recognize what an authentic life is – and isn't. A fixed mindset breeds inauthenticity because in order to please everyone, ignore constructive criticism, avoid challenges, and obsess about looking perfect, you have to play safe, play small, be judgemental and hide parts of yourself to live up to other people's expectations. This is what it feels like to live an inauthentic life.

HOW YOU'VE BEEN SHAPED BY THE WORLD AROUND YOU

We are constantly bombarded with messages that tell us happiness is found in material things. Most of our 'flaws' that apparently need fixing were conjured up by big corporations brainstorming ideas on how to keep women buying products in the name of self-love. Capitalism has created a 'perfect' image of a woman that is, in reality, unattainable.

Even though our insecurities may not be our fault, it is our responsibility to figure out a way to love ourselves and create our own truth. There comes a point in our life where we can no longer blame our parents, teachers, friends or society for our shortcomings and we have to take ownership of our life, our dreams, and our choices.

If you're not happy with the life you have right now, the good news is you can create a version that works for you, a version based on *your* truth and vision.

From the moment we're born, we're swimming in a massive sea of 'truths'. Unfortunately, it's often the dysfunctional 'truths' that stick in our heads. One of the keys to being Confident and Killing It is knowing what truths serve you and what truths don't.

When I started my personal growth journey and learned that growth was intentional and I had the power to define myself and my future on my own terms, it became clear to me that the narrative that I wasn't talented, skilled or creative wasn't loving or right, and didn't feel good, so I decided to let it go and create a new truth.

I put my limiting beliefs to the test and found out that everything I believed about who I was and what I was capable of was untrue. Today, my story is completely different, and yours can be too.

HOW TO CREATE YOUR OWN AUTHENTIC TRUTH

Here are five practical steps you can take to create your own authentic truth and build a strong foundation of confidence.

These steps are an integral part of the journey you're embarking on in this book and are fundamental to increasing your self-awareness and confidence.

STEP 1:
IDENTIFY AND ARTICULATE YOUR STRENGTHS

CONFIDENCE CHECK-IN: A LOOK INTO YOUR MIND

Time yourself for one minute and write down as many of your strengths as you can think of, then for another minute write down as many weaknesses as you can think of.

- Which came easier to you?
- Which do you have more of?

Knowing your strengths is arguably the most important aspect of building confidence and is often the most overlooked step.

Take a moment and think about what's going on in your head. If you know your weaknesses better than your strengths, it means you're operating from a place that feels negative and critical, instead of a place where you believe you're good enough.

Knowing your strengths doesn't just boost your confidence – it also helps you overcome fear and insecurities like imposter syndrome. Are you surprised you tend to feel like a fraud when you have no idea of what you bring to the table?

Sis, stop sleeping on yourself.

If you don't know what makes you unique, you will adjust to who the world says you should be – and that will always be smaller than your true potential.

Knowing your strengths doesn't just boost your confidence – it also helps you overcome fear and insecurities like imposter syndrome.

Here are five questions to help you articulate your strengths:

1. What do you naturally excel at?
2. What work energizes you?
3. What do people compliment you on or praise you for?
4. What do you do to add value to people or situations?
5. Think of a moment when you were proud of yourself. What strengths or skills did you demonstrate in that moment?

If you struggle to embrace your strengths, it's probably because:

You confuse strength with perfection.
Doing something well doesn't mean it has to be perfect. Perfection does not exist. You are human and just because you make a mistake once doesn't mean you have no strengths. Don't be too hard on yourself.

You compare your strengths to others and end up feeling like you don't measure up.
You don't have to be number 1 in the world to claim something as your strength. I used to think I wasn't creative because my creativity didn't look like painting, drawing, or playing an instrument (which my siblings were excellent at), but I am creative in my own way. Your strengths are your strengths in relation to you, your life, and your journey. There's enough room for all of us to have the same strengths; what makes us unique is how we apply them.

You think owning your strengths is arrogant.
You've likely been taught that humility equals smallness, so owning your strengths feels arrogant. But hear me clearly: disregarding or being in denial about your strengths is simply fake humility. It's not bragging if you did it – it's a fact.

Being aware of your positive traits is the first step towards building confidence. Once you know what you're good at, be intentional about using those skills. Embracing your strengths unlocks inner power. Neglecting your strengths feeds your insecurities. What choice are you making?

Your strengths are your strengths in relation to you, your life, and your journey.

STEP 2:
DEEP-DIVE INTO YOUR PASSIONS

The next step in discovering your authentic self is diving deep into your passions. Your passions are the things that energize you and set your heart on fire. They're your life's fuel.

I truly believe life is abundant and vast, and passion is the same. Passion is dynamic, so at different stages in your life, you will have different passions. Don't be so focused on finding one passion that you miss all the other joys around you.

Grace Beverley said it best in her book *Working Hard, Hardly Working*:

> 'We need to widen the scope of what passion means and live in a way where we insert smaller passions into the everyday, rather than try to fit the complexity of our everyday needs into a single passion.'

How is following your passions linked to confidence? When you care deeply about something, you're willing to take risks, learn and persevere. That sense of purpose fuels self-belief and action.

Passion fuels action. Action creates proof. Proof strengthens confidence.

Here are three questions to help you identify your passions:

1. What do you talk about? What type of conversations light you up on any day at any time?
2. What do you cry about? What's a pain-point or problem in

the world that upsets you so much you want to do something about it?

3. What do you daydream about? What do you lose time thinking about? When you think of your future, what joyful moments does your mind wonder about?

The answers to these questions will point to the things that make you feel alive, and when you live them out, they build your confidence. Playing small soon becomes very uncomfortable, and the drive within you begins to overpower the fear you feel.

Now I can already hear some of you screaming, 'BUT WHAT IF I HAVE TOO MANY PASSIONS?' My answer to that is, you're allowed to express and explore all areas of your personality. This is the art of authentic living. However, what it doesn't mean is that you turn every passion into a business idea and run yourself thin. Instead, look for common themes across all your passions and see how you can bring them into a cohesive whole. Passions aren't only topics like politics, travel, food and theatre. They can be more contextual, like problem-solving or social change.

Similarly to your strengths, engaging your passions unlocks inner power, while neglecting your passions breeds unfulfilment. You get to decide what kind of life you create.

Forgoing passion for money or the approval of others is never worth it in the long run. Creative expression is essential to your well-being, so think about how you use your free time. Don't spend your whole evening watching TV, then get mad at yourself for having no time to follow your passions. You have to make the time.

STEP 3: DEFINE YOUR VALUES

The third part of creating your authentic truth is unlocking fulfilment by defining your values and honouring them.

Values are defined as principles or standards of behaviour, one's judgement of what's important in life. When you feel there's something missing in your life, or you're lacking motivation, or feel unfulfilled or stuck, it's often because there's a value or set of values you're not honouring.

So, why are values important? It's because values:

- **Build self-trust**: Every time you honour your values, you prove to yourself that you can be counted on. Honouring your values builds self-trust. When you stand for what you believe in, it fuels authenticity and makes you unapologetically confident.
- **Help with decision making**: When you know what matters, you stop second-guessing yourself, you quit analysis paralysis and you move in the direction aligned with your true, authentic self. You also become less overwhelmed because now you can prioritize instead of trying to be everywhere and doing everything.
- **Create better boundaries and relationships**: Communicating our values shows other people how we want to be treated as well as what behaviour we find acceptable vs unacceptable. If you don't know your values, you don't stand for anything; you'll let people walk all over you and give people with the wrong energy too much access to your life.

Here are five questions to help you identify your values:

1. When do you feel most alive or 'in your element'?
2. Who inspires you and why? The reasons why people inspire you often reveal the values you hold.
3. If you could solve one problem in the world, what would it be?
4. What behaviours in others instantly frustrate or upset you? For example, if lying upsets you, integrity is a core value.
5. What kind of legacy do you want to leave behind?

Confidence grows when you show up as your true self, not a watered-down version. Living by your values helps you speak up, set boundaries, and be unapologetically you.

But there's a catch: *knowing* what's important doesn't mean you'll automatically *do* what's important. Wellness is important to me, but it's the thing I sacrifice as soon as life gets busy. So, in addition to knowing your values, you have to create time to honour them because one thing I know for sure is that compromising your values means compromising your true, authentic self, and that always has painful consequences.

CONFIDENCE CHECK-IN: DOING WHAT MATTERS

- Take a moment now and take stock of your life.
- Make a list of all the things that are important to you and track how much time you spend doing those things.

Make a habit of prioritizing tasks and activities that matter. That is true productivity.

Compromising your values means compromising your true, authentic self, and that always has painful consequences.

STEP 4:
UNLOCK YOUR POWER CIRCLE

Once you've identified your top strengths, passions and values, it's time to bring it all together to create what I call your Power Circle.

Your Power Circle is your zone of genius. It's your North Star and the core of your authentic self. When you live in alignment with your strengths, fuel your passions and honour your values, you unlock next-level clarity, confidence and purpose.

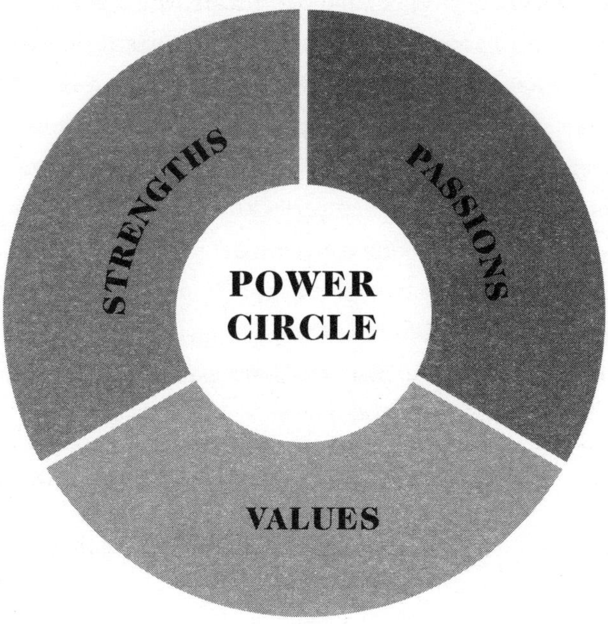

What you'll begin to notice as you explore your strengths, passions and values is that:

Everything you need to win in life is already within you.

#CAKIMANTRA

You already have the strengths you need to pursue that passion project. You already have values that align with your biggest goals. The Power Circle helps you spot the synergy between the three and shows you how to live from that place every day. For example, imagine someone whose top strength is **organizing**: they plan all the activities in the friendship group, they're also passionate about mental well-being, and deeply value **connection**. Their Power Circle might lead them to start wellness retreats for women recovering from burnout or join the mental health committee at work.

As for me, I have strong communication skills, I'm passionate about empowering women, and I value impact. When you put all that together, you get Confident and Killing It. That's why I've been able to create so much impact in a short space of time – no one can do it like me. That's my superpower.

Once you've identified your own Power Circle, look for ways you can live from that place every day. Is your current role in alignment with your Power Circle? Is there a business idea or community project you can work on that taps into all three?

Be intentional. When you live from your Power Circle, you become unstoppable.

Successful people know what they are good at doing, know what they love and get about the business of doing it.

The successful people you admire and look up to aren't necessarily smarter or more hardworking than you – they are strategic. They know what they are good at doing, know what they love and get about the business of doing it. No excuses.

That's how I went from an insecure people-pleaser to a globally recognized confidence coach. I stopped waiting for permission, tapped into my Power Circle, and owned my personal power.

STEP 5:
CREATE YOUR PURPOSE

Now it's time to think about how your personal power can be used for something bigger than yourself – this is your purpose.

Purpose is about being in the service of something bigger than yourself, and you can create your own purpose through your Power Circle. Notice I said 'create' purpose and not 'find' or 'discover'. No one is born knowing their purpose; purpose is something you create as you live authentically and intentionally. It isn't an end goal, it's active. It's a daily practice.

Purpose gives you a sense of meaning and direction. Your journey to building confidence and living authentically will have its ups and downs. Knowing your *why* makes you less likely to quit when things get hard. Purpose dares you to trust yourself even when you don't have all the answers or feel 100 per cent ready – and that trust is the bedrock of confidence. More on this in Chapter 9.

No one is born knowing their purpose; purpose is something you create as you live authentically and intentionally.

A word of caution: Serving others doesn't mean losing yourself. Don't neglect your needs to please the world, your family, or your partner.

Also, you don't have to be a role model or an inspiration to every single person. Stay true to yourself, help those you deeply care about, and use your gifts in the best way possible.

I want to end this chapter with one single message:

Autopilot ain't cute.

You owe it to yourself to be awake to your own life, know what sets you apart, recognize what you are good at doing, and realize that everything you need to win in life is already within you. Your starting place is good enough, but as you go through each moment, day and season, you're evolving and getting closer and closer to your truest, most beautiful, authentic self – and you'll be doing that until your last days.

So, keep an open mind as you read this book and begin to discover new parts of yourself. The more you know and accept your authentic self, the more you'll know and accept your sense of worth and personal power.

2

GETTING SASSY WITH THE MEAN GIRL IN YOUR MIND

As you become more intentional about being your authentic self and living from your Power Circle, your mind will often feel like a battlefield. Your newfound confidence and power will be in a tussle with your old thoughts and behaviours. One of the biggest confidence killers you'll come up against is the negative voice in your head. I call mine 'the Mean Girl', and that's the name I'm going to use here. She's that voice in between your ears that tells you you're not good enough, not smart enough or not pretty enough.

The Mean Girl says she's there to protect you, but all she ends up doing is stressing you out and making you doubt yourself. Let's change that!

Your mind is like a battlefield of conflicting forces. It usually works against you, but you can program it to work for you.

#CAKIMANTRA

HOW TO TAP INTO THE POWER OF YOUR MIND

Do you know you can actually *reprogram* your mind to be less negative and more positive? You can turn down the volume of the Mean Girl and turn up the volume of your Inner Cheerleader. Your Inner Cheerleader is a real ally. It can be a song, a person you admire, your grandmother's voice, or a positive mantra.

Your ability to reprogram your mind is thanks to your brain's 'neuroplasticity'. Science has confirmed that the brain is a dynamic organ, with the capacity to be shaped, trained and influenced in response to new information and life experiences. This completely challenges the excuses that people often give for not changing: 'I'm stuck in my ways' or 'It's just the way I am'. Change isn't easy, but it is always possible with intentionality and practise.

The biggest, most life-changing realization of my twenties was understanding the power of my mind and how to program it for success. In this chapter, I'm going to show you how to do the same in a very practical way.

YOU BECOME WHAT YOU BELIEVE

It's scientifically proven that our thoughts influence our feelings, and our feelings influence the actions we take. Our thoughts become beliefs when we think *and* act in accordance with them over and over again.

Believe you're worthy of your dreams coming true, and you'll go after them with relentless passion.

Believe you're bad with people and social situations, and you'll develop social anxiety. Believe you're worthy of your dreams coming true, and you'll go after them with relentless passion. Your beliefs either sabotage you or empower you. It's so important to be fully awake to how your mind works, and notice what you repeatedly think and say to yourself.

HOW TO WIN THE BATTLE IN YOUR MIND

Not every single thought about yourself is the truth about who you are.

We can't always control what thoughts pop into our heads, but we can control whether a negative thought is repeated so often that it turns into a limiting belief.

Not every single thought about yourself is the truth about who you are. Some are lies with a sprinkle of truth, some are straight-out lies, and some are actually the truth. It is your job to filter them and decide which ones you're going to keep as beliefs and which ones you're going to label as rubbish and bin.

The goal is not to get rid of the Mean Girl forever. A little bit of self-doubt actually keeps us grounded because it forces us to reflect, slow down, and acknowledge our imperfections. The goal is to notice the self-doubt, challenge it and then take action.

Confidence is not the absence of negative thoughts or self-doubt. Confidence is not feeling happy all the time. Confidence is *not* perfection. Confidence is about having a deep belief in yourself and your abilities despite the self-doubt. You've got to move past the fear and insecurity, and bet on yourself.

At 21, I made the life-changing decision that my default would no longer be allowing my Mean Girl to sabotage me but instead I would wake up every day and *choose love, self-belief and power*, because loving yourself is something you *learn* to do, not something you're born knowing how to do.

Confidence is not the absence of negative thoughts or self-doubt.

NEGATIVE THOUGHT DETECTOR

The Negative Thought Detector is a simple three-step practice designed to help you become curious about negative thoughts, change how you respond, and choose a different perspective.

Question 1: Curiosity

'IS THIS 100 PER CENT FACT OR AM I MAKING AN ASSUMPTION?'

If your thought is a fact, then fine; focus on what you can control and leave what you don't have the power to change.

However, if your thought is an assumption, then it can be changed. Let's look at a few different types of thought biases we all experience:

- **Mind reading**: Making assumptions about what others are thinking – for example, assuming everyone thinks you're awkward. Or assuming someone at work doesn't like you because they've not responded to your email.

- **Overgeneralizing:** Taking what happened in one experience and assuming it's the same for all future or past experiences. For example, one piece of negative feedback about your work means all your work is now terrible.
- **Musts and shoulds**: Having unrealistic expectations and putting pressure on yourself to be, look or feel a certain way. And then assuming you're a failure when you don't measure up.
- **Catastrophizing**: Always assuming the worst possible outcome without considering more likely and realistic possibilities.
- **Emotional reasoning**: Thinking that if you feel a certain way about an event, then it must be true. How many times have you felt you messed up an interview so badly, only to get a call telling you that you got the place?
- **Black-or-white thinking**: Thinking in absolute extremes: 'If I'm not 100 per cent good at it, then I'm terrible. It's all or nothing.'

Question 2: Compassion
'WOULD I EVER SAY THIS TO A FRIEND?'

Would you ever say to a friend, 'Don't speak up, you might say something stupid,' or 'Why are you so awkward with people? You're so cringe.'

You would *never, ever, ever* say these things to your best friend. So, give yourself some grace, and speak to yourself the way you'd speak to someone you love.

Question 3: Challenge
'DOES THIS THOUGHT SABOTAGE ME OR EMPOWER ME?'

Here's my rule of thumb:

If a thought sabotages you, bin it.
If a thought empowers you, run with it.
#CAKIMANTRA

Sabotaging thoughts belong in the bin because they drive you further away from your dream. Empowering thoughts elevate you. They encourage you to keep moving forward, and, most of all, they are who you really are.

So, when you question what your Mean Girl is telling you and you can see that it's an assumption, that you would never say that to a friend, and that it's sabotaging you, replace the thought with something more empowering, realistic and truthful, *based on your strengths.* Don't fake the positivity but instead take a moment to explore a more helpful perspective.

The moment I gave myself permission to make a different choice – a choice that is available to all of us – I activated my Inner Cheerleader, and a positive and powerful voice kicked in.

Getting sassy with the Mean Girl in your mind isn't about reciting overly positive 'You go, girl' affirmations that you found online. **This is about strategically gathering positive evidence of yourself (through your strengths and your wins) and using it to challenge your limiting beliefs.**

Confidence is about having a deep belief in yourself and your abilities despite the self-doubt. You've got to move past the fear and insecurity, and bet on yourself.

Whenever the Mean Girl shows up with her lies and false accusations, you kill those lies with the truth of who you really are.

The Negative Thought Detector is a quick and practical way to deal with negative thoughts on the spot when you don't have time for deep introspective thinking and feeling. However, for real confidence and to let go of more ingrained limiting beliefs, you'll need both practise and space to go deeper into how to manage and process not just your thoughts, but your emotions and actions too.

RIDING THE WAVE OF YOUR EMOTIONS

Emotions, emotions, emotions … I know some of you already want to skip the next few pages because … emotions? 'Ewww, don't do those.'

That was me too. In my mind I was *a strong independent woman*, so anything that didn't align with that had to be buried. But when I started my life-coaching training, I soon learned that being human isn't about only feeling happiness and ignoring everything else – being human is about feeling ALL your emotions. Emotions aren't 'good' or 'bad', they're neutral. They're just energy in motion.

E - M - O - T - I - O - N - S = energy in motion

Emotions flow in and they flow out. We experience a whole wave of emotions every day, and that isn't a bad thing. It's the meaning we give to our emotions that makes us embrace them or avoid them. The worst thing we can do for our growth is to expect only 'positive' emotions, because if our goal is only to be happy, then we are going to limit the richness of our life. Don't run from pain – sit with it. Yes, it's going to be hard, but in the end it will be worth it. Why? Because purpose can be created from pain.

Emotions aren't 'good' or 'bad', they're neutral. They're just energy in motion.

Adversity can reveal strengths you never knew you had. So, let's explore how difficult emotions can be teachers instead of a jailors. It's time for some practical application with The 3 A's.

THE 3 A'S

When things go wrong, don't beat yourself up about it or dwell on it for so long that it spills into other areas of your life. Try these steps instead:

1. **Acknowledge** how you're feeling.
2. **Articulate** what you're feeling.
3. **Allow** yourself to move forward.

STEP 1:
ACKNOWLEDGE HOW YOU'RE FEELING

This is simply accepting the fact that you feel a bit … meh. Acknowledgement is so important, because you can't process something if you don't even acknowledge it exists.

Life is a rollercoaster, not a straight path. It goes up and down, fast and slow, and sometimes it even feels like you're spinning upside down. Good mental health isn't perfect mental health. Emotions are complex, and we never just feel one single emotion. You can be an optimistic and positive person while also acknowledging your hurt, anger or fear. Start to notice your natural emotional patterns so you don't feel surprised by your mood swings. For example, understanding how different phases of the menstrual cycle affect your mood can help you stay confident when you're in a dip. Keep a journal, or try a menstrual tracking app like Moody.

STEP 2:
ARTICULATE WHAT YOU'RE FEELING

Once you've acknowledged that you're in a funk, start to find the words to express what you're feeling. Expressive writing can clear your mind's worries and free up resources in your brain to use on other tasks. It can lead to better sleep, a stronger immune system, and more self-confidence.[2] On the next page is a tool called the Wheel of Emotions, to help you put a name to what you're feeling:

---

2 Phelan, Hayley, 'What's All This About Journaling?', *The New York Times* (25 October 2018). https://www.nytimes. com/2018/10/25/style/journaling-benefits.html

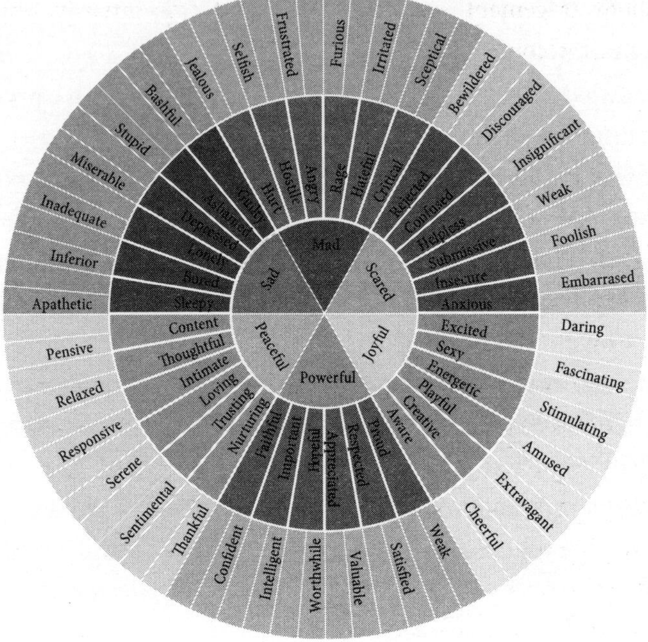

There's no right or wrong way to journal, but if you don't know where to start, here are a few ways:

Free Flow

Sit down, get still, breathe deeply, feel … then let it all out.

- Where in your body are you feeling emotional pain?
- What's going on in your mind?
- What's going on in your environment?

Dump all the different emotions or worries you're feeling and write without judgement. Just keep going, and if an intrusive thought pops in, welcome it and write it down too.

'I Release And I Welcome'

Make a list of all the heavy feelings you want to release. Start the list with 'I release ...'.

Then make a list of all the feelings you want to welcome. Start the list with 'I welcome ...'.

Once you've finished, meditate on the feelings you're welcoming, and visualize yourself filled with positive energy. Creating images of these positive and soothing associations can help release stress, regulate your emotions, and boost your energy.

Moving your body is also essential for releasing heavy emotions. I often do Yoga with Adriene's YouTube tutorial for anxiety and stress or attend a boxing class.

Exploring a Memory

Think about an experience or memory that brings up painful emotions, and then answer these questions:

- What thoughts did you have about this experience and what it meant to you?
- What negative emotions surface most often around it (like anxiety, shame or guilt)?
- How did you respond to the emotional pain? How were actions helpful and unhelpful to you?

- In what ways is the emotional pain a result of the unrealistic demands you place on yourself, others, and the world around you?

If journalling still isn't your thing and you prefer to speak to people, make sure you are speaking to someone you trust. See a proper professional if you need to. My rule of thumb is that if you're stuck in the odd rut here and there, be vulnerable and open up to someone you respect and trust. If it's something heavy that keeps coming up for you over and over again, then speak to a therapist or coach.

STEP 3:
ALLOW YOURSELF TO MOVE FORWARD

The great thing about rollercoasters is, no matter how crazy or scary the ride is, they keep moving forward until they reach the finish line. In the same way, when you feel that life is taking you on a wild ride, remember it doesn't end that way. Rest when you need to, ask for help when you need to, and then get back up and give yourself permission to move forward. A lot of us want to be resilient, but we don't want to go through the tough situations that actually cultivate resilience and strength. So, accept your 'negative' emotions as an opportunity to build resilience. The key is not to get stuck in them.

To start moving forward when you've been in a rut, get intentional about building your positive emotions back up. The 'P' in the PERMA model – the five pillars of well-being – stands for 'Positive Emotions'. Here are some things to try to start feeling good again.

Mindfulness Meditation

Practising mindfulness involves being in the present moment without worry and regret.

Box breathing is my favourite way of doing it:

- Place your left index finger on your right nostril to close it.
- Breathe in through the left nostril for four seconds.
- Hold your breath for four seconds.
- Release your right nostril and use your left thumb to close your left nostril.
- Breathe out of your right nostril for four seconds.
- Hold your breath again for four seconds.
- Release your left nostril, use your left index finger to close your right nostril.
- And repeat until you feel calmer.

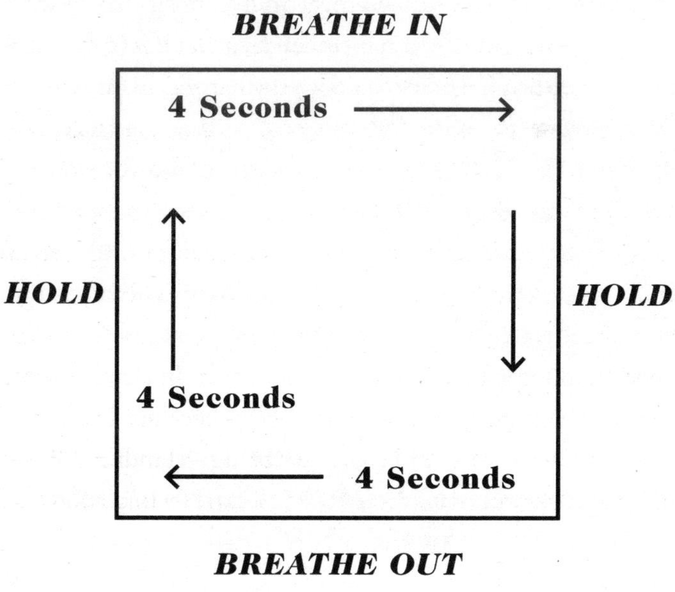

Get Intentional About What Brings You Joy

Make a list of all the things you love doing, then schedule in time in your calendar to do one of them every day. This will ensure any unmet needs that may be causing your low mood are prioritized.

Joy isn't just fun activities, you can also find it in:

- **Growth**: Learning a new skill, reflecting on your wins.
- **Meaning**: Honouring your values, helping someone, doing what truly matters.

Gratitude Journalling

This right here is an absolute game-changer! There's ample data to show that practising gratitude can lead to greater levels of happiness and better mental health.

Every evening, write down three to five things that went well for you that day, and as you remember them, lean into the positive emotions they bring. Focusing on what you have, instead of what's missing in your life, is the fastest way to change your mood.

If you've been suffering from a negative mind your whole life and haven't thought change was possible, I hope this chapter has inspired you to embrace your power and give yourself a fighting chance. You're not helpless. You are more than your anxiety and your trauma. When the Mean Girl shows up, get curious, challenge assumptions, and practise compassion.

You are more than your anxiety and your trauma. Emotions come and go, but your worth? That's *here to stay*!

3

REALIZING THAT YOU ARE CAPABLE

In the Introduction, we defined confidence as 'the belief that you are capable of succeeding in whatever you want to do in life and becoming whoever you want to be'. In this chapter, we're going to break that down and start exploring what believing in your abilities actually looks and feels like.

A part of you may be thinking, 'I see my potential, but am I really capable of making my dreams happen? Can I really own my own house? Can I really land my dream job?' Everything might feel so big and so overwhelming that you don't even know where to start.

It's easier to disqualify yourself from your dreams than it is to take the risk, go after what you want, see if you're capable, and potentially face the pain of rejection or failure if things don't work out as planned. When facing ambitious goals, you may feel you just don't measure up, but the truth is:

Knowledge and capability are not the same thing.

#CAKIMANTRA

Just because you don't know *how* to do something doesn't mean you're not *capable* of doing it. Just because you don't know *how* to achieve a dream doesn't mean you're not *capable* of achieving that dream. Read that again. Whatever you don't know can be learned. This is where a growth mindset comes into play.

A GROWTH MINDSET

Leads to a desire to learn and a tendency to embrace challenges and not expect life to be perfect, and persist in the face of setbacks rather than give up.

- Understand the importance of habits, and see hard work as the path to mastery.
- Learn from criticism without assuming the responsibility for pleasing everyone.
- Be driven by a strong sense of purpose and vision, and find lessons and inspiration in the success of others.

Right now, you might have a big dream, a dream you've not even told people about because it sounds so beyond you that they'll think you're crazy. I want you to know that you are not crazy. You are capable. So please stop disqualifying yourself from your dreams before you've had the chance to pursue them.

Just because you don't know *how* to achieve a dream doesn't mean you're not *capable* of achieving that dream.

LEARNING AND LEVELLING UP

Society says if you don't know how to do something, just 'fake it till you make it', but something about that didn't sit well with me, so I created a more empowering concept: Learning and Levelling Up.

This is where you acknowledge that you don't know it all or have it all, and that's OK! You acknowledge your limitations, but you know that the skills and knowledge you need to succeed can be yours with hard work, practice, learning and community support. Learning and Levelling Up is an empowering perspective because it gives you ownership of your life. Your shortcomings are no longer a reason for you to sit on the sidelines.

If you believe you're capable even when you don't have all the answers, you give yourself a chance. And one chance is all you need.

When you realize that you are capable, you believe you are worthy of making your dreams come true and you bet on yourself. When you give yourself a chance, there's still a possibility you might fail, but there's also a possibility you might succeed, so lean into that possibility.

Newsflash: There's no shame in saying, 'I don't know'.

We're all learning as we go along. Life is so complicated, dynamic and unpredictable that it's impossible to know everything. So be kind to yourself, because no matter how much you learn, there will always be something you don't know. This is why you can't wait until you've ticked all the boxes before you take action. You've got to learn a little, apply your knowledge, then learn some more. Everyone experiences self-doubt sometimes, or even imposter syndrome (see page 5), and I've seen some really smart people with low confidence, and that's because confidence is action-focused; it's not about how smart you are. You can have all the knowledge in the world, but if you never bet on yourself, take action, and apply your learning, you will not be confident.

When you tap into a growth mindset and create a clear mental picture of who you want to be and the life you want to live, something magical happens. You start to notice opportunities that you didn't notice in the past, you become excited by what you can achieve, and you begin to see the steps you need to take to level up:

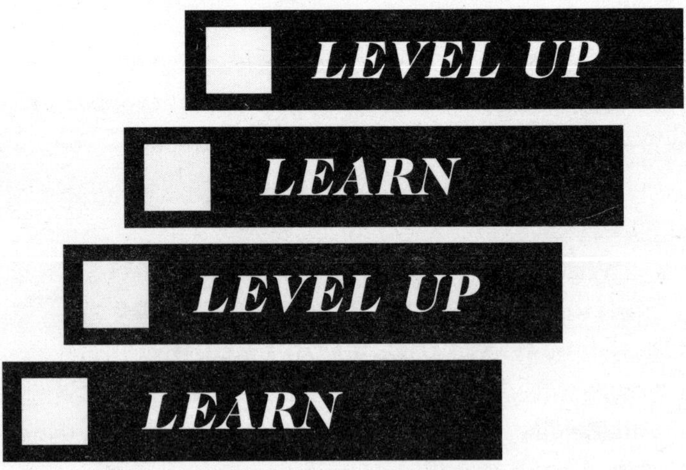

SEVEN STEPS TO REALIZING YOUR CAPABILITY

You're not going to attempt to take action on a dream if you don't think you're qualified in the first place. If you believe you're capable even when you don't have all the answers, you give yourself a chance. And one chance is all you need, so here are seven questions you can ask yourself to help you get more comfortable going after big, audacious and scary dreams:

1. **'What's the dream/goal that feels a bit scary?'** Always start by defining and writing out what the dream is. Don't just leave it as a thought in your head.
2. **'Is this dream in line with my Power Circle?'** If so, carry on to the next step; if not, then revisit your Power Circle and tweak the dream.
3. **'Why is this dream or goal important to me?'** Having an emotional connection with your dreams helps you feel more inspired and motivated to take action.
4. **'What internal resources do I have to potentially make this work?'** Reflect on your strengths, passions, values and skills.
5. **'What external resources do I have that I can make use of now and in the future?'** Reflect on your professional network, community, technology, government schemes, etc.
6. **'What three things can I start doing today/this week to get one baby step closer to my dream?'** Don't worry if this feels scary, we'll tackle the fear later on; just write it down.
7. **'What areas do I need to Learn and Level Up in to increase my chances of success with this dream?'** Once you've identified the knowledge or skill gaps between where you are and where you want to be, set goals to start working on them.

For example, completing a marketing course or learning another language so you can live abroad.

If your knowledge gaps feel overwhelming after completing this exercise, remember that a lack of knowledge isn't a lack of capability. It's the small, consistent steps that often lead to big, fundamental life changes. For example, if you want to become more financially literate and start investing, you can start by reading one article a day or listening to podcasts to learn key terms and concepts. Then you can join online financial literacy–focused communities like Female Invest to widen your knowledge and connect with like-minded people.

A lack of knowledge isn't a lack of capability.

We tend to overestimate what we can do in one year and underestimate what we can do in three years. One hour a day working on your personal growth is better than ten hours once in a blue moon. Focus on winning the day.

Finally, it's important to work towards a big vision while staying happy and grateful in the present. Our brain is more likely to achieve success when we are happy and feeling good about ourselves. So, enjoy the ride, and don't despise the days of small beginnings.

4

DITCHING THE WEIGHT OF PERFECTIONISM

When we're young, many of us are taught to be high-achievers and show up as our very best. This is healthy, as ambition fuels growth. But somewhere down the line in our adulting journey, we often turn into over-achievers, and the unhealthy traits of perfectionism and ambition kill our confidence. **But, in reality, perfectionism isn't about having high standards – it's about self-protection.**

Perfectionism is just a coping mechanism to avoid criticism, blame and shame. It keeps us stuck in fear instead of moving our life forward.

#CAKIMANTRA

Perfectionism is defined as 'a tendency to set excessively high and unrealistic standards for yourself and/or others'. Like any personality trait, it includes a whole spectrum of characteristics that vary from person to person. Let's look at five differences between being a high-achiever (pursuing a healthy standard of excellence) and being an over-achiever (pursuing perfection). If you see yourself in any of the negative descriptions, don't freak out. This chapter is about ditching the weight and learning healthier ways to pursue excellence without losing yourself.

PERFECTIONISM: THE HEALTHY AND UNHEALTHY TRAITS

So, are you a *high*-achiever or are you an *over*-achiever? Let's get into it!

When it comes to setting goals and targets …

- Over-achievers will often set their initial goals out of reach, with crazy deadlines that move them past the 'stretch zone' into the 'stress zone'.[3] It's one thing to go the extra mile, but it's quite another to overstretch yourself and enter a cycle of burnout, which is what pursuing goals often feels like for over-achievers.
- High-achievers also set high goals, but these goals are within reach, with deadlines that are realistic. They stretch themselves but know their boundaries and won't sacrifice their health in order to achieve their goals.

3 Heath, Nicola, 'Are You a High Performer or an Over Achiever?', INTHEBLACK, CPA Australia (1 April 2021). https://www.intheblack.com/articles/2021/04/01/high- performer-or-overachiever

When it comes to achieving their goals ...

- Over-achievers will prioritize outcomes over people, health, relationships and personal joy. They are laser-focused on the end result, and the way in which they go after the goal often outweighs the reward. They often feel frustrated when the goal takes a while to achieve.
- High-achievers focus more on the journey than the goal. They see the beauty in the process and understand that's where the real lessons of wisdom lie. They stay mindful and find fulfilment in the present moment while working towards their final destination.

When it comes to measuring their progress and defining success ...

- Over-achievers will accept nothing less than perfection. Any result that isn't an accomplishment of the original, overly ambitious goal is seen as a failure. They've either done it all or achieved absolutely nothing.
- High-achievers, on the other hand, will experience some level of satisfaction and pride in doing a great job, even if they didn't completely reach their original target. Rather than obsess over results, they see success as any step in the right direction and acknowledge that slow progress is still progress and worthy of celebration.

When it comes to reviewing their personal performance ...

- Over-achievers find it easier to spot their mistakes and tend to amplify their imperfections. They also internalize failure as something being wrong with them, wallow in negativity, and are highly critical of themselves. If they do happen to do something well, rather than feeling pride or joy in their accomplishments, they are simply relieved that they have not failed.

- High-achievers take pride in their accomplishments and celebrate their wins. They don't compare their performance to that of other people, so they tend to be more supportive of others' successes than over-achievers. When things go wrong, they don't let failure define them. Instead, they maintain a strong sense of self-worth, treat themselves with compassion, and reframe failure as a stepping stone to success.

When it comes to receiving constructive criticism from others ...

- Because a less-than-perfect performance is so painful and scary to over-achievers, they tend to see constructive criticism as a personal attack.
- High-achievers see constructive criticism as really valuable information and use it as motivation to grow, learn and level up. They don't feel that anybody is 'out to get them' and instead appreciate the openness and honesty of the feedback.

So, if you'd like to stress less and achieve more, ditching perfectionism is the best thing you can do for yourself.

CHOOSING VULNERABILITY

Brené Brown, a *New York Times* bestselling author and researcher pioneering the vulnerability discourse, describes perfectionism as:

> … the ultimate fear that the world is going to see us for who we really are, and we won't measure up. As a result, we end up walking around with a 20-ton shield, hoping it will protect us, but it actually stops us from being seen. Vulnerability, on the other hand, is the willingness to show up and be seen with no guarantee of the outcome. People often see vulnerability as a weakness, but vulnerability sounds like truth and courage. Truth and courage aren't always comfortable, but they are never a weakness.[4]

Admitting you aren't perfect, admitting you've failed, admitting that you are sometimes afraid takes a whole lot of courage, but the beauty of vulnerability is that you can be all those things and still see yourself as someone who is brave, strong and worthy of love.

When you embrace and speak up about what the world expects you to be ashamed of, shame cannot thrive.

You can use vulnerability as a superpower by embracing what the world expects you to be ashamed of. Then shame loses its power, and you gain yours.

---

4 OWN, 'Dr Brené Brown on Faking It, Perfectionism and Living Wholeheartedly | SuperSoul Sunday | OWN', (17 March 2013). https://www.youtube.com/watch?v=_ YeulUgWNp8

PRACTICAL VULNERABILITY

Now that we've looked at the power of vulnerability, let's look at how to get practical with it. We have to make the choice every day to let our authentic selves be seen by others and embrace all of who we are in order to live more fully.

Start From Within

Here are five questions to help you open up so you can have a deep conversation with yourself:

1. Why do I feel the need to be perfect, and who am I trying to be perfect for?
2. What am I afraid will happen if I'm not perfect?
3. Is the way I'm thinking and acting in alignment with my core values?
4. How do I hold space for my emotions and feelings?
5. What's worth doing even if I fail?

Take Risks and Start Before You're Ready

Putting yourself forward when you have no idea what the outcome will be is the height of vulnerability. Many of us want to wait until we feel ready, wait for confidence or a burst of courage before we act, but what we are really doing is hiding behind a need for control. Practising vulnerability means being willing to throw yourself in, take risks, and bet on yourself – even when you don't know exactly how it's going to go. One thing I know for sure is that the pain of regret is far worse than the pain of trying and failing. So, get started, because your dreams are waiting for you.

Examples of ways to practise vulnerability include:

- Asking to be paid more money.
- Saying 'I love you' first.
- Sharing an idea or dream with someone.
- Starting a new hobby.
- Speaking up on social media.
- Applying for a new job even when you don't tick all the boxes.
- Going to a dance or drama class with strangers.

Ask For Help

To a lot of people, asking for help is a weakness. But that perspective is not helpful because it often leaves you feeling overworked and overlooked. What if asking for help means you're a collaborative person? What if it means we're working smarter, because delegation lets you move faster? You can be strong and still ask for help. It's not all or nothing.

Get real with yourself for a second and think of an area in your life where you could do with some help. I used to be one of those 'It's quicker to do it myself' people, but let me tell you, learning to delegate and build a team was the best decision I ever made.

Openly Embrace Your Struggles

There is beauty in your strengths and your struggles. Actively acknowledging and sharing your struggles is a good way to practise vulnerability. Just as it's important to share your wins, it's also important to be transparent and share the lessons you've learned from your mistakes, failures, and dark seasons.

A word of caution, though: vulnerability isn't about sharing with everyone all the time. You've got to set boundaries with it. Share when you feel safe. Know what and when to share with people close to you, and know what and when to share with your wider community. This is very subjective, but I prefer to share when I'm in a healthier head space and have identified the key life lessons from my struggles. I never share a struggle publicly without sharing what I've learned from it. That way, I no longer feel that my story owns me; instead, I own the story.

If you feel a bit of regret after you've been publicly vulnerable, that's all part of it. Let the emotion come and go, and know that the focus is less on what you shared and more on the fact that you were brave enough to be seen and heard by others in a way that feels authentic.

Be Kind to Yourself

Being kind to yourself is a form of vulnerability. Being open to loving yourself unconditionally, regardless of what you look like, regardless of how messy your mind is and the mistakes you've made, is vulnerability. Being kind enough to forgive yourself for poor decisions you've made in the past and give yourself another chance is vulnerability.

In my teens and early twenties, I struggled with acne. After spending years being super conscious of what I looked like, I started to look into my eyes in the mirror and say, 'Tiwa, I love you.' It's an empowering practice.

TO PRACTISE SELF-COMPASSION, YOU COULD ALSO:

- Prioritize your self-care.
- Write a love letter to yourself or to a specific insecurity.
- Look into the mirror regularly and read out daily mantras to stop comparison from stealing your joy (see also pages 97–103).
- Set boundaries.
- Reset yourself by completing these sentences:
  - '[Your name], I love you for ...'
  - '[Your name], I forgive you for ...'
  - '[Your name], I'm proud of you for ...'

Write a list of all the things you forgive yourself for, then turn the page, and start a new chapter.

NURTURING BODY CONFIDENCE

We can't talk about ditching the weight of perfectionism without addressing the pressure women and girls feel to have the 'perfect' body. In a world that thrives on our insecurities, being unapologetic about your body is one of the greatest revolutions – and one of the hardest challenges.

Body positivity is about loving your body as it is and rejecting unrealistic standards.

Body neutrality is about taking appearance out of the equation and valuing what your body can *do*, not just how it looks.

Body confidence blends both. You can defy the status quo and celebrate the body you have while also appreciating all the amazing things it does for you. Confidence doesn't mean you'll feel great about your body every single day. It means not letting insecurity hold you back from living your life. There is more to you than what you look like, and your body should be seen as a part of you, not as defining all of you.

So, the next time you feel the need to hide behind perfectionism to avoid criticism, judgement and shame, remember that the goal in life isn't to be liked by everyone, but to be your true, authentic self. Ditching perfectionism doesn't mean lowering your standards. It means choosing courage over control, progress over paralysis, and authenticity over approval.

You won't always get it right. You won't always feel confident. But when you embrace vulnerability, honour your body, and stop measuring your worth by perfect performance, you take your power back.

5

TURNING PROCRASTINATION INTO PRODUCTIVITY

Procrastination isn't a laziness issue. It's a mindset issue. It's scientifically proven that our thoughts, emotions and actions are all connected. Our ability to act or procrastinate all comes down to the thoughts in our head.

For example, perfectionism and procrastination tend to go hand in hand. Fearing failure as they do, perfectionists will sometimes worry so much about doing something imperfectly that they become immobilized and fail to do anything at all.

Focusing on avoiding failure doesn't lead to success – it leads to procrastination.

Let's say you have a deadline coming up at work for a pitch deck you need to submit. If you're procrastinating, you're probably thinking:

- 'I'm not creative enough to do this. They'll probably hate my ideas.'
- 'I hate speaking in public. I always mess up my explanations.'

- 'Why did they even give me this project? I'm not the best person for this job.'

All those thoughts will make you dread working on the pitch deck, and you'll just keep pushing it back because the negativity is so overwhelming.

On the other hand, when you think positively about yourself, you see your capabilities, take action, and build confidence, which creates momentum to keep going. You're not lazy, you're not lacking talent, you're not a bum; your negative thoughts are just running your mind, so you need to flip the script.

Think about a task you've been procrastinating over. Are your thoughts about it negative or positive? I'm 100 per cent sure they are negative, which is why you keep getting stuck.

Here are some ways to flip the script and turn procrastination into positive action:

- From 'I have to' → 'I get to'
  Reframe tasks as opportunities, not burdens. Gratitude fuels motivation.
- From 'It has to be perfect' → 'Done is better than perfect'
  Progress builds momentum; perfection stalls it.
- From 'I'll start when I feel ready' → 'Action creates readiness'
  Readiness is an illusion. Waiting for motivation keeps you stuck. Action often creates it.
- From 'I might fail' → 'I'll learn as I go'
  See failure as a stepping stone to success, not proof that you shouldn't try.

- From 'I have no time' → 'I'll make time for what matters'
  Align your actions with your priorities, not your excuses.
- From 'This will take forever' → 'I'll just give it ten minutes'
  Break overwhelming goals into small, achievable actions. Starting small bypasses the mental resistance to begin.

PROMISES, PROMISES …

A big part of being confident is keeping the promises we make to ourselves. Every time we tell ourselves we'll take action and we don't, we're breaking the trust we have in ourselves and sending a loud message to the universe that our dreams aren't worthy. If we don't trust ourselves, we won't bet on ourselves, won't believe in our capabilities, and definitely won't unlock our full potential. 'I'll do it tomorrow' isn't just a casual phrase to throw around – say that enough times and before you know it, it's been five years and you still haven't started.

A big part of being confident is keeping the promises we make to ourselves.

If you feel that you've broken the trust with yourself, take steps to rebuild it, just as you would any other relationship. Start by making smaller promises to yourself that you can keep. It will take time, but stay committed, because it's you and you for the rest of your life, so learning to trust yourself should be your number one priority.

MOVING BEYOND BUSYNESS TO PURPOSEFUL PRODUCTIVITY

We live in a world that glorifies busyness. The longer your to-do list, the more worthy you're supposed to feel. But here's the truth: being busy isn't the same as being productive. You can hustle all day and still get nowhere that matters.

Purposeful productivity is about alignment, not busyness. It's about using your time and energy on what truly matters to you and activities that leave you feeling alive, not depleted.

When you shift from chasing busyness to choosing purpose, you stop measuring your life by boxes ticked and start measuring it by impact made. That's real productivity.

You're a human, not a machine. Your worth isn't based on your ability to produce work. The mere fact that you're alive and breathing means you matter.

#CAKIMANTRA

DEFINE PRODUCTIVITY ON YOUR OWN TERMS

Remember when I said that part of being Confident and Killing It was knowing what societal rules to accept and reject? Well, this is one of them. Productivity doesn't have to mean doing excessive work to the point of burnout. You can redefine it in a way that works for you. For some people, especially if you live with ADHD (Attention Deficit Hyperactivity Disorder — a condition that affects focus, impulse control and time management), 'traditional' productivity rules feel impossible to follow. Redefining productivity on your own terms is even more important, because your brain needs strategies that make focus easier and procrastination harder.

I'd like to invite you to choose a new definition, one that is based on prioritizing what matters.

$$\frac{\textbf{Doing What Matters}}{\textbf{Time Spent}} = \textbf{Productivity}$$

It's not about the quantity of boxes you're ticking, but the quality of the activity you're doing. Does it honour your values? Does it lead to real growth and progress? Does it contribute to your overall well-being and fulfilment?

Another thing I love about this definition is that 'doing what matters' looks like different things to different people. Doing what matters will also look like different things in different seasons.

So, productivity can look like:

- Rest and relaxation.
- Turning off your phone to focus.
- Taking action on your goals.
- Clearing out your inbox.
- Going on holiday.
- Running errands.
- Going through the mail.
- Getting together with your colleagues to brainstorm solutions.
- Sacrificing going out to meet your deadlines.
- Spending time with people you love.
- Asking for help and delegating.

And the list goes on and on. This definition of productivity also allows you to maintain a good work–life integration because you can tap into your inner wisdom and prioritize what your body and mind need at that specific time. Notice I said work–life *integration* and not work–life *balance*.

Productivity doesn't have to mean doing excessive work to the point of burnout.

Work–life integration feels more like a braid: we weave different aspects of our life together to make a single thread. A little bit of work, then some play, then some adventure, then some work, then some wellness, and so on and so forth. That's what productivity can look like too. But here's the catch – weaving only works if you're intentional. It takes self-awareness to know what your mind and body need in each season, and discipline to make choices that honour those needs instead of falling back into busyness.

FIND YOUR FLOW

If you want to be productive, pay attention to what gives you energy and what drains you. You can do this by making a list of all the tasks you have to carry out in the day and then writing down how you felt during and after the day. Once you track your energy levels over time, you can prioritize doing more of what gives you energy, because that will lead to an optimum state of flow. Flow is a state of utterly blissful immersion in the present moment. When you're in flow, you are doing deep-thinking work, you lose track of time, and you are fully immersed.

The second letter in the PERMA model (refer to page 7) – the five pillars of well-being designed by positive psychologists – is 'E' for 'Engagement'. As humans, we have a natural inclination to busyness, because when we're not doing anything we tend to feel bored or useless, so working gives us a sense of worthiness. However, as I explained above, the key is not to be busy doing work you couldn't care less about. Real productivity is being engaged in work that truly absorbs and inspires us.

In *Daring Greatly*, Brené Brown says, 'We don't have to be perfect, just engaged and committed to aligning values with action.'

Perfection isn't the goal – feeling alive is. Aligning your actions with the things that matter to you and to your strengths is what *really* makes you feel confident, productive, successful and valuable. It's also my number one tip for balancing a full-time job and side hustle. Having a full-time job that supports the skills, knowledge and passions you need for your side hustle will help you stay in flow.

It's difficult to spend your evenings and weekends building a business when you're unfulfilled for eight hours every day. You're also more likely to achieve your goals when your brain is in a positive state. So, if you want to be more productive working on your side hustle, find a full-time job that energizes you during the day, so you can maintain momentum at night.

Real productivity is being engaged in work that truly absorbs and inspires us.

Now, some people are able to use hating their job or current situation as motivation to work harder, and it's true that sometimes we have to do work we don't like because it gets us closer to where we actually want to be. For example, taking a less exciting role at your dream company gets your foot in the door and means you can apply for something better later on. But being stuck doing work you hate, with no end in sight, isn't beneficial for your growth or your soul.

FOCUS ON YOUR OWN LANE

Comparison feels a lot like driving a car and looking everywhere but ahead of you. It generates productivity guilt. Let's say you wake up at 9 a.m. and go on Instagram and see someone has been up since 6 a.m. and has gone to the gym already. You start feeling guilty that you're not working hard enough and worry that you're going to get left behind. Comparison is the biggest driver of low self-esteem. It will make you feel either superior or inferior to others and neither of those states is healthy.

Comparison is the biggest driver of low self-esteem. It will make you feel either superior or inferior to other people, and neither of those states is healthy.

When you define productivity on your own terms, someone working while you're resting doesn't mean you're losing. Rest is productive if that's what your body needs the most in that moment.

LOCK IN SMALL WINS TO GAIN MOMENTUM AND BE CONSISTENT

Talent is cool, but consistency is what really takes you over the finish line. When you have a big mountain to climb, break it down into baby steps and focus on winning the day. A lot of the time we procrastinate because the task feels so big and overwhelming;

we disqualify ourselves before we've even attempted it. This is especially true if you have ADHD. The brain struggles with 'big, vague tasks', so breaking things down into bite-sized tasks isn't just helpful, it's essential.

Just win today.

That's my mantra whenever I'm working on a challenging project that could become overwhelming.

Once you get started, you'll build momentum and make progress. For many of us, motivation actually comes once we start, not before. Seeing ourselves making progress fuels us to keep going, because we know our effort isn't in vain and a reward is just around the corner.

Another #CAKIMantra that helps me celebrate small wins is this:

Slow progress is still progress.

#CAKIMANTRA

'Slow progress is still progress' ditches perfectionism and allows us to embrace the journey rather than obsess over the finish line.

TURN YOUR TO-DO LIST INTO A GET-TO-DO LIST

If your to-do list gives you anxiety because it feels like you have so much to do in so little time, use this powerful technique to align it with your values.

Take the values you identified on pages 17–18 and assign every task on your to-do list to a personal value of yours. This helps you move it beyond a task you 'have to' complete to a value you 'get to' honour. For example, I don't *have* to record a podcast episode; I *get* to record an episode and impact someone's life in a positive way (the core value being impact). I don't *have* to meditate; I *get* to meditate and take care of my mind, body and soul (the core value being wellness).

MANAGE YOUR TIME AND PRIORITIZE YOUR TASKS

The Eisenhower Matrix is a really great tool for deciding how to prioritize tasks. Prioritize what's urgent and important, delegate what's urgent but not important, schedule a time to do it if it's important but not urgent, and if it's not urgent and not important, then remove it completely from your to-do list. Grouping tasks is a great way to make them feel more manageable and get the ball rolling.

Don't forget, your environment also plays an important part in being productive and following through with new habits. If you have ADHD or struggle to focus, set yourself up for success by making sure your environment supports the new changes you're trying to make. If you want more focus, make it hard to become distracted – delete the apps, turn off notifications, clean your room, and declutter your workspace. A messy room = a messy mind. Next, make it easier to focus by making your get to-do list the night before and blocking out focus time in your calendar. Your environment has to agree with the goal you are pursuing.

Make sure your environment supports the success you want.

So, remember, when it comes to turning procrastination into productivity, be aware of the connection between your thoughts, feelings and actions. Make sure you know why the tasks you do are important to you and how they align with your values.

Finally, self-compassion is a much more powerful motivation tool than self-criticism. Both may get you to your final destination, but using self-criticism and being hard on yourself as a form of motivation feels like going through life with a ton of bricks on your back. But self-compassion puts a spring in your step and forms a very strong foundation for you to start betting on yourself.

6

STARTING TO BET ON YOURSELF

Fear is a negative prediction of the future, not a truthful projection of it. We think, 'What if I mess up? What if they laugh at me? What if they don't love me? What if I fail? What if my dream never comes true? What if they ghost me?' Then, as we begin to visualize everything going wrong, our body gets tight and we feel nervous, anxious and worried, and then we retreat. Sound familiar? Meanwhile, none of these things have actually happened yet.

In the last few chapters, we've looked at how you can get better at believing in your worth and your capability, and not waiting to be perfect before you start. Once you overcome the mental hurdle of perfection and procrastination and start taking baby steps, after a while, as you gain momentum, you will get to a point in your life where you have to make a big decision. Maybe it's time to overcome your commitment issues and allow yourself to be loved, or it's time to make the leap from a full-time job to your side hustle. Whatever it is, you've been going along on your journey, but now you're at a cliff with no bridge over the chasm. You can either take a leap of faith or settle down at the edge, never making it to the other side. If you've been choosing to settle at the edge of the cliff up until now, then wakey, wakey, it's time to pack up that tent and get going! The next few pages are about to help you face your fears and take that leap.

THE POWER IN FACING YOUR FEARS

Let's start with why fear seems to have so much power over us. Fear feels so paralysing. It feels heavy, it feels overwhelming, it slows us down to the point of no action.

Fear has saved many lives, but it has also killed many dreams. A lot of people think, 'If I feel afraid, that's a sign that maybe I shouldn't do it.' And in some situations that makes sense, but when it comes to goals, dreams and opportunities that help unlock our potential, we can't take that approach.

Confidence isn't an absence of fear. Every single one of us, no matter how confident we may look on the outside, has felt afraid at some point in our lives. The key difference between people who reach their potential and those who don't is that they feel the fear, master it, and keep moving forward.

Feel the fear, master it and keep moving.

When we experience fear, it feels so heavy, so overwhelming, so real. But all this time, it's just one big 'what if' – one big possibility that may or may not happen. **Fear tricks us into believing that the worst outcome is the only outcome. The truth is, it's not.** There are many more possible outcomes that we need to acknowledge and explore, however much fear will try to persuade us otherwise.

Rehearsing the worst outcome over and over again guarantees the worst outcome. Why? Because your subconscious mind obeys the command of your most *dominant* thought. The subconscious is the part of your mind that runs in the background. It stores your beliefs, habits and emotional memories, and it influences most of your decisions without you even realizing it. When you constantly visualize or think about failure, your brain starts filtering reality to confirm it. You start spotting risks instead of opportunities, hesitating instead of acting, and sabotaging your own progress because that's what you have instructed your mind to do.

This is why fear of failure often leads to inaction, and inaction guarantees failure. So, if you keep thinking, 'What if I fail, what if I fail, what if I fail?', you are 100 per cent going to fail because the fear of failure stops you from even trying. You will fail if you do nothing. If you try, you might fail, *but* you might succeed. Failure is a possibility, not a certainty. By not trying, you are giving yourself a 0 per cent chance of achieving your goal.

- What's the best way to find out if people will buy your product or service? *Put it up for sale.*
- What's the best way to find out if you'll get a promotion? *Apply for it.*
- What's the best way to find out if you will enjoy taking a trip on your own? *Book it.*

The future is yours to invent.

The only way to find out what the future holds is to invent it by taking action now. You have to lean into the positive possibilities of your life rather than letting fear keep you in a vicious cycle of rehearsing the worst possible outcome and not even trying.

The three biggest fears I see in the women I've coached are:

1. **Fear of failure:** 'What if it all goes wrong?'
2. **Fear of inadequacy:** 'What if I'm not good or capable enough to succeed?'
3. **Fear of judgement:** 'What if I show up online and get backlash?'

Imposter syndrome also feeds off fear. You're afraid to fail because you think if you do, other people will think you're a fraud or a fake. You're afraid to ask for help because you think other people will think you're weak and don't really know what you're doing. All of these fears are linked with our deepest human desires to succeed, feel seen, feel heard, and know that we matter.

Did you know that your biggest fears are often in direct correlation to the things you want the most? In a boxing match, a heavyweight fights a heavyweight, not a lightweight. They want to go after their match. In the same way, your biggest fears and doubts go after your biggest dreams and desires. They go after the things you want the most. Once you become aware of that, you'll stop seeing fear as a sign to retreat and instead you'll see it as a sign that you must move forward. You'll begin to ask yourself, 'What else could this mean? What other possibilities exist?'

We need to stop seeing failure as a wholly irreversible negative experience. If you bet on yourself and try something new and it doesn't work out, you now have more knowledge because you know what works and what doesn't, and can make better decisions next time, which, in all honesty, is a success.

My question to you is: How long are you going to let fear mess you around and hold you back in life? Aren't you tired of feeling stuck and overwhelmed? Both faith and fear require you to believe in something you can't see. It all comes down to the choice you make. Let's choose to master fear once and for all.

REFRAMING FEAR

Confidence isn't an absence of fear – confidence is feeling the fear but doing it anyway.

#CAKIMANTRA

Here's a Reframing Fears Technique (RFT). It'll help you break down your fears, so they no longer have power over you. By the time you have gone through these six steps, the fear shouldn't feel so scary anymore, and you should begin to manage it instead of letting it manage you.

STEP 1:
NAME THE FEAR

You can't master what you don't first acknowledge. Don't group fears – write down exactly what you're afraid of. Big fears feel overwhelming; mini-fears can be managed. Break them down until you can see the truth.

My client Anita wanted to become a full-time entrepreneur. Her broad fear was 'What if I'm not successful?' But inside that were mini-fears: 'What if I let my parents down?' 'What if I can't find clients?'

We focus so much on how scary action feels that we forget to ask: *What's the cost of inaction?*

STEP 2:
FIND GRATITUDE

What hidden gift or lesson does this challenge bring? Gratitude shifts fear from an enemy into an opportunity. Reframing fear starts with gratitude. Even in scary situations, ask: *What can I be grateful for here?* Seeing how your current challenge can add value to your life is a powerful way to spin things around.

Anita feared letting her parents down, but she was grateful they cared about her future. Being in this situation added value to her life because it pushed her to have an honest conversation with them, in which she would learn that sometimes disappointing others in order not to disappoint yourself was OK. The conversation was an opportunity to practise how to defend her dreams to people who didn't get her vision.

STEP 3:
PLAY THE WHOLE MOVIE

We focus so much on how scary action feels that we forget to ask: *What's the cost of inaction?*

Avoiding failure doesn't give you success. What happens when you stay in your comfort zone? You don't grow.

What happens when you don't grow? You feel unfulfilled, you feel stuck, you lack motivation and ambition.

What happens when you feel unfulfilled? You begin to hate your life, hate yourself and feel depressed.

It's a long movie on a downward spiral. The next time you feel afraid, play the full movie out in your head and see if that's the path you want your life to take. Probably not.

If Anita avoided fear, she'd stay in a job that drained her, procrastinating and living an unfulfilled life. Ironically, the very thing she feared – disappointing her parents – would happen anyway.

The consequences of giving into fear and retreating far outweigh the momentary pain you might feel by pushing through the pain and learning to master it.

STEP 4:
VISUALIZE WHAT YOU WANT

If fear is what you don't want, focus on what you *do* want.

Grounding yourself by focusing on what you would rather be thinking and feeling (in the present moment) instead of worrying about what you don't want to happen (in the future) can really help calm your nerves.

Write out your ideal situation in the present tense and replay it in your mind.

Anita wrote:

'I am making my parents proud by betting on myself. They see the impact of my idea and encourage me to pursue it.'

Ground yourself in positive possibility, not panic.

STEP 5:
TAKE A SMALL STEP TODAY

Fear shrinks when you act. Start with baby steps, just one task, then build momentum.

For Anita, this meant:

- Sitting her parents down for an open conversation.
- Finalizing her business plan.
- Researching case studies for her idea.

Confidence is practice. And like anything we practise, we get better over time. So, the more you act, the less power fear holds. As you go through life, new fears will spark new opportunities to build confidence.

STEP 6:
CREATE A BOUNCE-BACK PLAN

What if the fear comes true? Well, prepare to bounce back. Creating a bounce-back plan will help you feel more confident to take the risk. Look at your strengths and how you overcame similar fears in the past. Pay attention to the skills you have within you and external support that can help you get back on your feet.

If Anita failed, she could draw on her determination and communication skills, and seek support from mentors. Fear tells us we won't cope. But remember, everything you need to win in life is already within you.

When our biggest fears become a reality, like freezing during public speaking or starting a business and then running out of money, we may be quick to label it as a failure. But after looking at what successful people have in common, I can tell you with certainty that it's better to face your fear, try, fail, and bounce back than it is to make excuses and never start. You can go from failure to success, but you can't go from excuses to success. More on this in the next chapter!

If you think failure defines you, think again. You are not your failures.

Failure is an event. It's something that happens to you, it's not who you are.

#CAKIMANTRA

You can *experience* failure, but you can never be a failure. Failure has a start and end date, so don't let it define your whole life. Redefine it. Embrace it. Use it.

You only have one life. Don't let fear bully you into playing small. Tap into your inner greatness, visualize the outcome you want, create a bounce-back plan, and take baby steps forward.

The world needs you. The world needs your ideas. The world needs your light. You can **F**ace **E**verything **A**nd **R**un, or you can **F**ace **E**verything **A**nd **R**ise. The choice is yours.

You can *experience* failure, but you can never be a failure.

THE GOLDEN RULES WHEN YOU FEEL LIKE GIVING UP

On the path to your ambitious goals, reality won't always match your expectations. Some days will feel heavy, some paths will feel harder than planned. The temptation to give up will be real.

But here's the truth: successful people are the ones who didn't quit when it got hard.

When the destination still matters but the journey feels tough, remember these golden rules:

REMEMBER YOUR WHY

Reconnect with why the goal matters. How does it fulfil you? How does it impact others?

The fourth pillar of the five pillars of the PERMA well-being model is 'M' for 'Meaning'. Studies have shown it is very important to feel that the work we do is consistent with our personal values and beliefs. When we believe our work is worthwhile, we feel a general sense of motivation and confidence that we are using our time and our abilities for good. There is also evidence to show that people who belong to a community and pursue shared goals are happier than those who don't.[5]

So, if you feel the work you're doing isn't in alignment with your purpose, values and beliefs, you will give up easily when things get

---

5 Madeson, Melissa, 'Seligman's PERMA+ Model Explained: A Theory of Wellbeing', PositivePsychology.com (2 April 2022). https://positivepsychology.com/perma-model/

hard because there's no sense of direction, no vision and certainly no motivation. This is why creating your Power Circle was one of the first concepts we explored. When you're living in alignment with your strengths, passions and values, betting on yourself and seeing the journey through are much easier.

The message in you is more important than the fear you feel.

#CAKIMANTRA

So, the next time you feel fearful, anxious, or ready to give up, remember your why. Remember one person who needs your message, your product or service. The world needs you. Your voice, your ideas and your contributions are all bigger than the fear you feel.

REMEMBER BAD SITUATIONS ARE NOT PERMANENT

When things are going wrong, it's hard to see the light at the end of the tunnel. We often feel as if the bad situation or challenge is permanent and pervasive, but it rarely is. It's often only one area in life that's difficult – not our whole life. Worrying won't make the problem go away; in fact, worrying is like actively praying for the worst possible outcome.

More importantly, if you give up in the middle of the storm, you 100 per cent guarantee that your dreams won't come true. So, learn to rest, process your emotions, and rethink your strategy instead of giving up completely. Slow progress is better than no progress. Crawling out of a challenge is better than sitting in it feeling helpless. Be grateful for any small improvement and be proud of how far you've come.

REMEMBER TO SPEAK UP AND ASK FOR HELP WHEN YOU HIT A ROADBLOCK

Imposter syndrome will make you feel afraid to ask for help because society has told us that successful people do it all on their own, but that's a lie. Asking for help when you get stuck doesn't mean you're a failure. In actuality, it creates opportunities for you to learn and level up. It creates opportunities for you to show those around you that they are needed and valued.

Worrying is actively praying for the worst outcome.

Now, many corporations value people who can take the initiative and solve problems, so when you do go and ask for help, make sure you've at least attempted to find a solution. No one has all the answers, and no one can do it all on their own, so when things get tough, make sure you have a strong community or team you can lean on – a group of people who will encourage you to keep going and cheer you on.

REMEMBER HOW FAR YOU'VE COME

A lack of experience when pursuing new paths or being stretched beyond your comfort zone can trigger feelings of fear and inadequacy. In those moments, it's essential to remember your previous accomplishments and all the transferable skills you've picked up along the way.

Your skills, knowledge and achievements all count as evidence that you can handle future challenges. No employer, job title or challenge can take them away. When you step into something new, you're not starting from scratch – you're starting from experience. And if the challenge is brand new? Lean on your ability to learn and level up.

KNOWING WHEN IT'S TIME TO QUIT

Encouraging you to never give up isn't romanticizing non-stop hustle. **It's about ensuring you do not surrender to defeat when the destination matters but the journey feels tough**. If the struggle is temporary, or fear is the only thing telling you to stop, you must push through and reclaim your power.

Quitting, on the other hand, can be an empowered, strategic choice. It's looking at a goal or situation and realizing it no longer aligns with your values or is costing you more than it's worth. It's the self-awareness to say, 'This isn't for me anymore, and I choose a better path.' Maturity is learning to accept your losses and walk away, instead of pouring more time and resources into a situation or person that's no longer serving your authentic self.

For example, you might want to consider quitting in some of these circumstances:

- If pursuing your goal is making you very unhappy and coming at the cost of your mental, physical and emotional health.
- If the only reason you haven't already quit is because you're worried about what other people will think.
- If you're the only one putting all the energy and effort into

a relationship, you'll need to accept you aren't a match and walk away.

- If the idea of walking away brings you peace, quitting so you can change paths is a good idea.

If it's fear or fatigue talking, reset and push through. If it's misalignment or a shift in your deeper purpose, let it go. Quitting doesn't make you weak; sometimes quitting is the smartest, boldest move you can make. The difference lies in *why* you stop and *what* it means for your bigger vision.

No matter how ambitious the goal, there will be moments when giving up feels easier. That's when these golden rules become your anchor. Stay rooted in purpose. Remember that hard times are temporary, and your past wins are proof you can keep going. No one wins alone, so build a support system you can lean on, and trust your intuition. Push through fear but walk away from misalignment. Growth is messy and hurdles are inevitable, but hang in there because you deserve to see your hard work pay off.

In the coming chapters, we're going to look at how you can get better at internalizing your success and keeping track of your accomplishments so when fear and imposter syndrome creep in, you remember what you're capable of.

Your skills, knowledge and achievements all count as evidence that you can handle future challenges.

7

LET YOUR BOUNCE-BACK BE STRONGER THAN YOUR SETBACK

So far, we've looked at internal confidence killers such as self-doubt, fear, imposter syndrome, and perfectionism, and by now you have the tools and the mindset to win those mental battles. In this chapter we're going to explore external confidence killers and how to bounce back when your confidence has been knocked. Your belief in yourself can be impacted by the environment you're in and other factors outside your control, like rejection and negative criticism. We've learned that confidence is a practice, so if it can be knocked, it can also be rebuilt. Let's get into it!

When 'bad' things happen to you, the lens through which you view them has the power to influence the action you take. Have a look at the kind of perspectives people tend to have in the midst of challenging situations in the chart on the next page:

VICTIM VIEW	CREATOR VIEW
It's permanent. Life will never be the same again.	It's temporary. It's just a season, it will pass.
Everything is bad.	It's just this one area of my life.
Nothing is in my control. I'm helpless.	Some things might not be in my control, but I'll focus on what I *can* control.
I must be a bad person for all of this to be happening to me. I'm not worthy of good things.	I am always worthy of good things. Sometimes bad things happen to good people.

Victims see situations as permanent, pervasive, and out of their control. When they have a negative experience, they discount all their previous successes just to focus on this one negative moment, and they feel defined by it. They accept it as their fate and replay it over and over again in their mind.

Creators, on the other hand, understand that life happens in seasons and that most challenges are temporary. When they have a negative experience, they don't discount all their previous successes, but learn from their mistakes.

So, the next time you find yourself in the middle of a storm, take a step back and look at how you're viewing the situation. A victim view leads to a dead end. A creator view gives you hope, and where there is hope, there is the opportunity to move forward and come out the other side stronger than ever.

REBUILDING YOUR CONFIDENCE AFTER IT'S BEEN KNOCKED

Here are five keys to coming back stronger once your confidence has been knocked:

1. ONE NEGATIVE PAST SITUATION DOESN'T DEFINE YOUR WHOLE LIFETIME ... UNLESS YOU LET IT

Failure, discrimination, rejection and abuse are things that happen to us – they do not define who we are. Your worst moments are not your identity; they are a moment in history. You have the option to let go and not carry that weight for the rest of your life. Learn to make peace with your past by accepting what you can't change and carrying the lessons forward instead of the baggage. See the situation as a source of wisdom rather than a source of shame. You are the author of your story and you have the power to define and redefine your life, over and over again. This is easier said than done, so if you're struggling to let go of something in the past, don't be afraid to get professional help like therapy. There's no shame in it.

Loving yourself enough to get the help you need is a beautiful act of bravery.

2. YOUR WORTH IS INTRINSIC – NOTHING AND NO ONE HAS THE POWER TO TAKE IT FROM YOU

You matter simply because you exist. Your worth doesn't depend on external things like a degree, money, a job, or who you know. People don't give you worth – you are born with it. So, when you experience rejection or a lack of validation, don't internalize it as something being wrong with you. Sometimes, bad things happen to good people. Regardless of what your life looks like right now, you are always worthy of good things.

3. YOUR OPINION OF YOURSELF MATTERS MORE THAN WHAT OTHERS THINK OF YOU

Growing up, you may have been told that you weren't good enough, weren't smart enough, or there wasn't anything special about you. If you grew up with very little encouragement or have had a very negative teacher, partner or manager who wore you down, you may be feeling the weight of all those limiting labels. But guess what? Never let people who only know a part of you define the whole of you. Those people may only have seen your limitations, but you owe it to yourself to uncover your potential, lean into your strengths, and create a new narrative for yourself. Your opinion of yourself carries more weight than what others think, so make sure you've got a good opinion!

Never let people who only know a part of you define the whole of you.

A big takeaway at this point is that there will be people in the world who don't like seeing you shine or be ambitious and they'll try and 'humble' you, but don't let them. No one knows you like you know yourself. No one knows your potential like you do.

The more you love yourself and believe in your capabilities, the less space you have to care about what other people think of you.

#CAKIMANTRA

So, if people try to crush your dreams with their negative words, the best response is to bounce back stronger than ever and kill 'em with consistency, determination and drive.

4. THE WAY PEOPLE TREAT YOU IS NOT A REFLECTION OF YOUR WORTH

If you've ever been discriminated against or hated on, you'll know how painful it feels and how easy it is to begin to question your worth. One thing I learned very early on is that the way people treat you is not a reflection of your worth, but actually a reflection of their own internal perspective and feelings about themselves. Someone who low-key hates themselves is unable to show you love. You'll never see a genuinely confident person being a hater in the comment section. Trolls are typically cowards hiding behind a false sense of security and significance. They'll try to tear you down for a moment of fleeting power, but no one has the power to take your worth away. Don't let people who don't matter, matter too much.

5. REJECTION DOESN'T MEAN YOU ARE A REJECT

Similarly to failure, rejection is something you experience. It is not your identity. One of the biggest and quickest ways to kill your confidence is to internalize rejection as something being wrong with you. If someone says 'no' to you, it doesn't have to mean you're not good enough. Here are three healthy ways to reframe rejection:

1. The Timing Wasn't Right

If you're seeking a work opportunity and get rejected, ask when a good time could be and then try again.

2. The Opportunity Wasn't Right

When one door closes, it's usually because there's something better coming your way. Getting rejected can be a blessing in disguise. Rejection can even be a form of protection and also redirection. Don't be disheartened, keep knocking on the door until the right one opens.

3. You Need A Bit More Time To Grow

No one is perfect and we're all a work in progress so, even though you might feel 100 per cent ready and sure that you can handle something, other people may need to see you succeed and grow a bit more before they have the confidence to bet on you and give you a chance. Again, don't take it personally. Be consistent and keep going, and before you know it, they'll be back again. As I always say:

When people don't give you opportunities, create your own!

#CAKIMANTRA

4. Bonus Point: If You Think You Need Closure To Move On, Think Again

Many people spend months, even years, waiting for closure before they can move forward. They wait for an apology that never comes, an explanation that would somehow make the pain make sense, or a conversation that would neatly tie up the loose ends. But here's the truth: waiting for another person to validate your pain or give you the 'right' words often leaves you stuck in the very situation you want to leave behind. In reality, the decision to move on is yours alone.

When you accept that you may never get the apology, the clarity, or the justice you think you deserve, you free yourself from relying on someone else for your healing. You stop making your peace conditional on their actions and start reclaiming your own power.

Moving on doesn't mean forgetting what happened or pretending it didn't hurt. It means deciding that your future matters more than the unanswered questions of your past. Let's use the 3 A's from Chapter 2 to process some unfinished business.

1. **Acknowledge** the grief, the anger and sadness. Yes, relationships are amazing, but breakdowns really hurt. Be still for a moment, and feel your feelings, because that's the only way to start healing.
2. **Articulate** the specific losses you're experiencing – for example, the loss of memories, the loss of the laughter and joy that person brought you, the loss of future plans that will never come to pass, the loss of their love and support, etc. Acknowledge that you have lost these things with this specific person, but that you haven't lost all of these things forever. New memories and new friendships can always be made.
3. **Allow** yourself to move forward by forgiving the person, forgiving yourself and then writing down what you most deeply need, even if you don't feel entitled to it. Not from that person specifically, but what you need to flourish and move forward from yourself.

STRENGTHENING YOUR SUPPORT SYSTEM

Yes, Ms Independent, I'm talking to you. You can be the most confident person on your own, but without the right support system, your confidence can only take you so far. Being independent and having a strong support system aren't mutually exclusive. Numerous studies show the impact that positive social relationships have on our mental and physical health.[6] Our relationships are such

---

6 Moeller, Robert W. et al., 'Emotional Intelligence, Belongingness, and Mental Health in College Students', *Frontiers in Psychology*, 11 (2020). DOI:10.3389/ fpsyg.2020.00093.

a fundamental part of our well-being that they've actually been designated as the third pillar of the PERMA model for achieving ultimate wellness and fulfilment – 'R' for 'Relationships'. Good relationships can reduce our rates of anxiety and depression, and lead to higher self-esteem and longevity.[7]

Another persona of imposter syndrome is the 'Soloist'. Soloists are people who prefer to do everything on their own because they see asking for help as a sign of weakness. They feel the need to work way harder than everyone else, which often leaves them in a place of severe burnout and stress. They tend to believe people will judge them if they don't come across as having all the knowledge and capabilities they need for their job, so they prefer not to ask for support and do it all on their own out of fear. But there's a catch: if you're a soloist, you think you're winning by doing it all on your own, but actually, life is hard – and when you burn out from overworking and trying to juggle everything, you're less likely to perform at your best and then you end up in a vicious cycle of low self-esteem and imposter syndrome. Not cute.

Self-love isn't a substitute for experiencing love and belonging.

The truth is there's no award for trying to do it all on your own. When we've been knocked down and it feels like all hope is lost,

7 'Relationships in the 21st Century: The Forgotten Foundation of Mental Health and Wellbeing', Mental Health Foundation (May 2016). https://www.mentalhealth. org.uk/sites/default/files/Relationships-in-21st-century- forgotten-foundation-mental-health-wellbeing-full-may-2016.pdf

having a community that cheers us on can give us a renewed sense of purpose and belonging, which motivates us to get back up again.

Bear in mind there's no one way to do community. It can be online, in-person or a mix of both. It doesn't have to be a huge crew; it can be just a few friends and confidants who care about you.

Humans are social creatures, and self-love isn't a substitute for experiencing love and belonging. When we have a good support system, we feel safe enough to take risks and actions that allow us to build confidence. On the other hand, if we're surrounded by toxic people who don't believe in us or tear us down with their words, it plants weeds of self-doubt that kill our potential.

Let's look at some red flags and green flags when it comes to relationships, so you'll know the types of people to stay clear of and the ones to surround yourself with.

THREE SIGNS OF UNHEALTHY RELATIONSHIPS THAT WILL KNOCK YOUR CONFIDENCE

1. **The person you're in a relationship with is obsessive:**
    - They want to be the centre of attention in your world, and at the same time they want you to be their be-all and end-all. They come across as very possessive.
    - They get upset when you don't prioritize their needs above yours, and they often want you to sacrifice your goals and opportunities for them.
    - They aren't that supportive of your wins, as it takes the spotlight away from them.

2. **They're consistently negative:**
    - These kinds of people often sow doubts in your mind about yourself and your abilities. They say really mean things to you when they're angry and use their words as a weapon to tear you down.
    - They belittle you and tell stories or jokes at your expense. They're very critical and pessimistic about everything you do. Being around them often drains your energy.
    - They put very little effort into the relationship, but expect you to go the extra mile for them.

3. **They're controlling:**
    - They have an image of who you should be, and when you don't measure up to that image, they make you feel terrible about yourself.
    - You often need to become someone else in order to make them happy. If you feel you can't be your true, authentic self around someone, that's a real red flag.
    - They rarely let you express your feelings and often make you feel you're overreacting or doing too much when you're simply being yourself.

THREE SIGNS OF HEALTHY RELATIONSHIPS THAT WILL BUILD YOUR CONFIDENCE

1. **They support your independence:**
    - People who give you space to live life on your own terms are keepers. They understand that sometimes you will need to prioritize your personal needs over theirs and that's OK.

- They don't make you feel bad about setting boundaries and don't take your independence as a sign that you don't love or need them.

2. **They support your potential:**
   - They use their words to build you up instead of tear you down. They are your biggest cheerleaders, they encourage you to go after your goals and help you see positive traits in your life that you don't even see in yourself.
   - They give you space to flourish and are inspired by your success instead of feeling jealous of it.

3. **They support your needs:**
   - They love you the way you want to be loved, not the way that's most convenient for them.
   - They give you space to communicate your needs and actively create an environment where you feel loved and protected. They listen when you speak.

Once you've identified the signs, you've got to learn to set boundaries with the confidence killers and get intentional about building your support system. To do that, you've got to invest in the relationships around you.

Humans don't form strong bonds over perfection, we form bonds over authenticity and vulnerability, so don't just talk about how amazing your life is, be honest and open up about some of your troubles to people you trust and share what you're learning from the challenging experiences. There's a clear line between 'misery loves company' and bonding over a shared experience. If your conversations are only ever about what's going wrong, how you're a victim or not good enough or you're seeking sympathy, then that's not authentic vulnerability.

Finally, being a positive, supportive and encouraging person goes a long way. People might forget what you've said but they'll never forget how you made them feel. Actively supporting someone's dreams is magnetic, as is showing up for them and bringing positive energy, and it's very likely they'll reciprocate in turn.

If you struggle to build genuine connections with people, use some of the practical tips I've shared in this chapter. Also, take personal responsibility for whatever healing you need to do to open yourself up to love and friendship again.

Bouncing back from setbacks isn't easy, so if you're reading this now, congratulations – you've survived 100 per cent of the challenges that have come your way, and those challenges have helped grow you, not break you.

Now it's time to shift the focus from overcoming challenges to actively succeeding on your own terms.

8

KILLING IT! SUCCESS ON YOUR OWN TERMS

When you think of success, what's the first thing that comes to mind? Money? Fame? Followers? Titles? Power?

For the longest time, success for me was all about numbers. Now, in theory, this view of success made sense because when I looked at all the people the world called 'successful', they were wealthy and had power and influence, so naturally I strived for the same thing. After a while, though, I started to notice that this 'success' never felt enough. Success that focuses on numbers never leaves you feeling satisfied, because there is always the possibility of more. Another downside of this view of success is that it feeds off comparison, because there will always be someone with a better number than you.

As an ambitious woman, success is important to me. A lot of us want to be successful, and it's not a crime to want that, but our definition of success has to go beyond money, power and fame for it to really mean something.

A woman who is Confident and Killing It must learn to define success on her own terms. She must learn to rely less on the world for validation and make her own choices that bring her deep fulfilment.

#CAKIMANTRA

A confident woman must learn to operate from a place of wellness, purpose and passion, and not define herself by material possessions, financial position or a culture that is actively working against her liberation. In this part of your journey, you'll learn not to let the world's superficial definitions of success rob you of the deep pride and acceptance you should feel for yourself. You'll learn what a healthy and empowering version of 'Killing It' could look like, and you'll get the opportunity to create your own.

The final element of the PERMA five pillars of well-being model is 'A' for 'Accomplishment'. Psychologists have concluded that to 'achieve well-being and happiness, we must look back on our lives with a sense of accomplishment: "I did it, and I did it well."'[8] Creating and working towards goals helps us look forward and build hope for the future. People who look back at their lives with a sense of accomplishment feel more optimistic and confident about their future because they know if they did it before, they can do it again. This is why it's so important to experience some level of success in your life. Even if you

8 Madeson, Melissa, 'Seligman's PERMA+ Model Explained: A Theory of Wellbeing', PositivePsychology.com (2 April 2022). https://positivepsychology.com/perma-model/

might not be where you want to be yet, or even if there are so many people ahead of you, everyone is worthy of success. So, if your definitions of success and failure make you feel insecure, change them.

So, if your definitions of success and failure make you feel insecure, change them.

Let's look at what happens when you follow the world's definitions. Success on anyone else's terms other than your own will leave you feeling inferior to others and exhausted by the effort to keep up.

We know we shouldn't compare ourselves to other people, yet we still do it. That happens because a lot of the time we aren't even aware of it. It's one of those things we do on autopilot. So, if we have any real chance of tackling this thief, we need to become more aware of its tactics and create our own comeback for it.

STOP COMPARISON STEALING YOUR JOY

In Chapter 2, you learned how to reframe negative thoughts and turn limiting beliefs into more empowering ones. That's exactly what we're going to do here with comparison. We're going to question the lies, ditch them, and create a new truth.

When Comparison Says …

'LOOK AT HOW TERRIBLE YOU ARE AND HOW PERFECT THEY ARE …'

You can challenge it by saying, 'No one is perfect, and I embrace the beauty in my strengths and struggles.'

Say it out loud.

Why is this true? It's true because you never know what's going on behind the scenes. For the majority of the time, what people show you online and in person is a curated version of themselves. It's simply a highlight reel and not the full picture. So, comparing the worst of yourself to the best of someone else isn't even a fair comparison.

Your insecurities are a part of you; they aren't the whole you.

#CAKIMANTRA

Get curious about all the things you are capable of rather than dwelling on all the things you're lacking. There is beauty in your strengths and your struggles. We tend to know our struggles all too well and forget that there are strengths to be explored and acknowledged. Get practical by making a list of all the things you love or appreciate about yourself and reflect on them regularly.

When Comparison Says ...

'LOOK HOW SUCCESSFUL THEY ARE, THEY'RE WAY AHEAD, AND YOU'RE SO BEHIND ...'

You can challenge it by saying, 'Someone winning doesn't mean I am losing. I am grateful for where I am while I'm on the way to where I'm going.'

Say it out loud.

Why is this true? It's true because the beauty in life is really in the process, not at the finish line. There are 8 billion or so people on Earth – there's no way we can all be at the exact same point in our journeys. Some will be ahead of us and some will be behind, but what really matters is that we're better than who we were yesterday.

So, remember, it's not you against the world. Your biggest fear shouldn't be that someone else is better than you. Your biggest fear should be that you had the opportunity to grow and evolve, but never seized it.

Get practical by celebrating your big and small wins using the Confident and Killing It Monthly Wins Tracker. The MWT is a tool you can download for free at confidentandkillingit.com/shop It encourages you to track your small and big wins every month, with visibility of the whole year, so you can see your journey. This tool is powerful because whenever we feel we're not making progress, or comparison is getting the better of us (which happens a lot), we can remind ourselves of how far we've come.

When you're consistent with sowing your seeds, what's meant for you will never miss you.

#CAKIMANTRA

The harvest is coming.

When Comparison Says …

'THEY BEAT YOU TO IT, THEY'RE ALREADY DOING IT WELL, THEY'RE MORE POPULAR THAN YOU ARE, THERE'S NO POINT IN EVEN TRYING …'

You can challenge it by saying, 'No one has walked the same path as me. My story is unique and I'll own it. Plus, there's enough room for all of us to thrive.'

Say it out loud.

One of the things I love most about having a growth mindset is believing that there is enough room for everyone to be successful. If you operate in spaces where no one wants to give you a seat at the table, build your own!

If you're not up for starting your own thing, you can always look for companies or environments that value your insight and experience.

Get practical by writing down key moments in your life that have shaped you and why. This will remind you of moments that have made you the unique individual you are today. And if you want to launch something but you're afraid that no one will care, speak to your potential customers, find out what their needs are, where the gaps are, and then build together with them.

When Comparison Says …

'EVERYTHING COMES SO EASILY TO THEM, LOOK HOW HARD YOU HAVE TO WORK AND STRUGGLE …'

You can challenge it by saying, 'I don't know what opportunities, knowledge and support they've had, so instead I'm going to focus on investing in my own growth, my creativity and my confidence.'

Say it out loud.

Why is this a fact? Because, unless you're God, you actually have no idea how much or little work someone has put in behind the scenes to get to where they are now. So, before you compare your Day 1 to that of someone who has been in the game ten years longer than you, or before you forget about someone's privilege and only look at their fancy opportunities, take a moment and focus on your own goals.

Get practical by listening to podcasts and interviews, reading books, and hearing the full stories of people you admire and the journeys they've been on.

If life still looks easy for them, find out about the behind-the-scenes systems, processes, habits and possible privileges that have benefited them. And remember: 'Someone winning doesn't mean I am losing. I am grateful for where I am while I'm on the way to where I'm going.'

When Comparison Says …

'IF YOU DON'T GET THE SAME THINGS THAT EVERYONE ELSE HAS, THEY WILL JUDGE YOU OR EXCLUDE YOU FROM THE GROUP …'

You can challenge it by saying, 'My goal isn't to be liked by everyone – my goal is to be my true, authentic self.'

Say it out loud.

Why is this a fact? The truth is, if people really like you for who you are, they won't care about what material things you have or don't have. Clout-chasers only care about what being friends with you gives them access to – and this isn't real friendship. So, if friends cut you off because you can't afford the same lifestyle they have and they don't want anyone messing up their appearances, then be very grateful to be out of such a toxic environment. Any relationship built on material things won't last.

Get practical by reflecting on your values and the things that really matter to you. Plus, use the tips about relationships from Chapter 7 (see pages 88–93) to take stock of the people in your life who are really in your corner.

RECAP: DAILY MANTRAS TO STOP COMPARISON FROM STEALING YOUR JOY

- 'No one is perfect, and I embrace the beauty in my strengths and struggles.'
- 'Someone winning doesn't mean I am losing. I am grateful for where I am while I'm on the way to where I'm going.'
- 'I don't know what opportunities, knowledge and support

they've had, so instead I'm going to focus on investing in my growth, my creativity and my confidence.'

- 'My goal isn't to be liked by everyone – my goal is to be my true, authentic self.'
- 'If they are winning, I can win too. Their success is a sign that it is possible for me too.'
- 'There is enough room for everyone to thrive.'
- 'If opportunities can go to them, opportunities can come to me too.'
- 'No one has walked the same path as me. My story is unique – I just have to own it.'
- 'Everything I need to win in life is already within me. I just need to wake up to it.'
- 'I will not doubt my greatness, and I will not be scared of my potential.'
- 'My success isn't defined by numbers.'
- 'I can trust the divine timing of my life. My best days are still ahead!'

The only time comparison makes sense is when you use it as fuel to motivate you to be better. If your comparison sounds like 'If they can do it, I can do it too', then it's healthy. Checking in on what other people are doing can give you creative ideas, help you read the room and give you a feel for what's going on in the world. It can even give you a vague idea of what to expect on your own journey.

When in doubt, always ask yourself if a thought feels empowering or sabotaging and remember the #CAKIMantra:

If it sabotages you, bin it.
If it empowers you, run with it.

#CAKIMANTRA

HOW TO REDEFINE SUCCESS ON YOUR OWN TERMS

Now that you have the tools to navigate comparison, it's time to break the rigid box of expectation surrounding what success looks like.

The moment I realized I was defining success all wrong was when I came across this quote from the poet Maya Angelou:

'Success is liking who you are, liking what you do, and liking how you do it.'

So powerful, yet so simple. Nothing about numbers, nothing about popularity, nothing about wealth.

It also got me thinking about how real success is about honouring your values rather than ticking boxes. Is it success if you're making money but hate every moment of your job? Is it success if you have to constantly sacrifice your health to reach your goals? I'll leave you to answer that.

Now, I know this is easier said than done, and the Nigerian in me is asking, 'Is self-love going to pay my bills?' But I wouldn't share anything with you that I personally haven't seen results from.

Is it success if you have to constantly sacrifice your health to reach your goals? Confidence isn't an absence of fear; confidence is feeling the fear but doing it anyway.

#CAKIMANTRA

The 'Killing It' in Confident and Killing It is less about capital gain and more about self-actualization. It's not about being a boss and climbing to the top of a ladder or going to extreme lengths to progress 'at all costs'.

I can't tell you exactly how you should define success, because at the end of the day, it's quite personal and there isn't only one way for a woman to be successful. However, since finding a definition that helped me feel more autonomous and patient with myself as I navigated life, I've done some more research and curated a list of three elements that can help you form your own healthy definition of success.

Here are some perspectives to consider when it comes to defining success on your own terms:

CHOOSE IMPACT AND QUALITY OVER POPULARITY AND QUANTITY

Success isn't about how much money you make. It's about the difference you make in people's lives.

– MICHELLE OBAMA

PRIORITIZE YOUR VALUES OVER SOCIETY'S EXPECTATIONS

> **To live the lives we truly want and deserve, and not just the lives we settle for, we need a Third Metric, a third measure of success that goes beyond the two metrics of money and power, and consists of four pillars: well-being, wisdom, wonder, and giving.**
>
> – ARIANNA HUFFINGTON

CHOOSE CONSISTENT GROWTH OVER ONE-HIT WONDERS

> **Dreams are lovely. But they are just dreams. Fleeting, ephemeral. Pretty. But dreams do not come true just because you dream them. It's hard work that makes things happen. It's hard work that creates change.**
>
> – SHONDA RHIMES

Hard work beats talent when talent doesn't work. Everyday wins build up to powerful, transformational change. Don't miss out on those small miracles because you're fixated on one big magical moment. Success comes from the small actions you repeat every day, not from big moves once in a while.

Success is about so much more than money and fame, and there's no one way to be successful.

The same thing applies when you're 'manifesting' success. Some people think this is just about thinking positive thoughts, saying, 'I want, I want, I want,' and then sitting back and waiting for the universe to deliver a big moment of success. That's not quite how it works. Manifesting success is about intention followed by action, and then faith. You believe in positive possibilities, you believe you deserve good things, and then every day you do something to take you one step closer to that dream. And while doing that, you don't obsess over the how and when of it happening. You don't obsess over the timeline or the exact outcomes. You set the intention, show up, play your part, trust the process, and then have faith that it will all work out for you.

Nature does not hurry, yet everything is accomplished.

– LAO TZU

I hope this chapter inspires you to ditch mindless striving and instead opt for prioritizing your well-being and fulfilment and knowing yourself well enough to do what works for you. Success is about so much more than money and fame, and there's no one way to be successful. A stay-at-home mum can be 'Killing It', a recent grad can be 'Killing It', the CEO of a Fortune 500 company can be 'Killing It'.

If your definition of success makes you feel exhausted, stressed or like a failure, change it. Your life, your rules, your pace – you can define success in a way that works for you, because you are worthy of being and feeling successful. Don't wait for someone else to validate you, and don't compare your wins to someone else's, because comparison will steal your joy. Protect it instead by focusing on your lane, being proud of the person you're becoming, and honouring the gifts and passions within you.

In the next chapter, we'll look at how we own and celebrate our success, because even after most of us have stopped obsessing over numbers, we still struggle to acknowledge our greatness. It's time to start celebrating your accomplishments.

9

EMBRACING YOUR MAIN CHARACTER ENERGY

Welcome to my favourite chapter, where you'll learn how to show up and speak up confidently in all areas of your life. In case you don't know, you are *that girl*! You're an icon, you're a legend, you're the whole table – plus the snacks. If you want to stop playing the supporting role in someone else's life and step into being the main character in your own life, then we're about to make that happen.

In the previous chapter, you defined success in your own way; now it's time to fully embrace it. Embracing your main character energy is about living out your purpose, and owning your voice, your accomplishments, and your personal story. Here, you'll learn how to communicate your purpose and value, whether in your career or your relationships, so you can create an aura that exudes confidence and a personal brand that attracts opportunities.

Articulating your value – and then learning how to communicate it with confidence – are so important, because you can be the most skilled and talented person in the world, but if you struggle to project a sense of certainty in your abilities, people will tend to overlook you. There is nothing more frustrating than being a hidden high-achieving woman.

CLARIFYING YOUR PURPOSE

When we embrace main character energy, it isn't about being loud for attention. It's about showing up, using your voice, your gifts and your story to make a difference.

Purpose is what makes your confidence matter.

As you learned in Chapter 1, purpose isn't handed to you. You don't need anyone else to validate your existence. Purpose is something you create for yourself. All I suggest is that you build it on the foundation of your strengths, passions and values.

Purpose is about connecting your life to something bigger than yourself, aligning your gifts with a mission that makes the world better. For me, that anchor is my faith. My purpose is to love God, love people, and use my gifts to make an impact that honours Him. For you, it might be family, creativity, justice or community. The key is the same: when you find your *internal why* and connect it to the *external who*, you unlock a sense of direction that gives your confidence real meaning.

- **Your Internal Why** → What drives me? What fuels me from the inside out?
- **Your External Who** → Who benefits when I live this out? Whose life gets better because I showed up?

This blend of inner fire and outer impact is where purpose comes alive.

Now it's your turn. Use the sentence structure below to write a short purpose statement that combines your why and your who. Don't overthink it – purpose isn't static, it evolves as you do. Get something down today, and allow yourself to refine it as you grow.

'My purpose is to . . . *[your internal why / what drives you]* so that . . . *[your external who / who benefits]*. As a result of . . . *[core action / your work]*, they experience . . . *[positive change]*.'

THE CREATIVE BABE

'My purpose is to *tell stories that inspire hope* so that people *feel seen and understood*. As a result of my art, they experience *connection, empowerment, and the belief that their voice matters.*'

THE CORPORATE BABE

'My purpose is to *be a leader who uplifts others* so that the *women around me see what's possible for them too*. As a result of how I show up at work, my team experiences *confidence, collaboration, and a culture of excellence.*'

THE BUSINESS BABE

My purpose is to *use my creativity and courage to turn ideas into impact* so that *others feel inspired to chase their own dreams*. As a result of my *business*, people *experience innovation, empowerment, and products that make their lives better.*'

OWNING YOUR VOICE

The second part of embracing your main character energy is about owning your voice. Regardless of where you are on your journey, being a confident communicator is essential.

GETTING SASSY WITH NEGATIVE THOUGHTS

A lot of people struggle to speak up because of the negative thoughts they have about what will happen when they do. These often sound like:

'What if I say something wrong or stupid?'

'Everyone here is smarter than me, my opinion really doesn't matter.'

'What if people judge me or laugh at what I've said?'

Ever said any of those to yourself? Yup, we've all been there. Time to challenge those negative thoughts using the Negative Thought Detector from Chapter 2 (see also pages 28–31).

Let's take 'What if I say something wrong or stupid?' as an example.

Question 1:

'IS THIS 100 PER CENT FACT OR AM I MAKING AN ASSUMPTION?'

If you can think, 'What if I say something wrong?', you also have the option of thinking of the positive possibility: 'What if I say something right?'

Question 2:
'WOULD I EVER SAY THIS TO A FRIEND?'
Think of the advice you would give a friend who was nervous about sharing one of her ideas, and then give that advice to yourself. Be your own cheerleader.

Question 3:
'DOES THIS THOUGHT SABOTAGE ME OR EMPOWER ME?'
Telling yourself you're going to say something wrong or stupid stops you from speaking up. In this case, a more empowering thought could be: 'My opinions matter and I deserve to share my ideas. If I say something wrong, I am only human, and I'll learn from my mistakes.'

Your mind is a battlefield of conflicting thoughts. Your negative thoughts are likely to be your default, but it doesn't have to be that way. Ditch the ones holding you back and create empowering thoughts you can believe instead.

THE 3 V'S OF COMMUNICATION
Once you've overcome any mindset barriers to communicating confidently, you can then move on to the physical elements of showing up confidently.

The 3 V's are the three most important elements to think of when it comes to being an impactful communicator. They are visual, vocal, and verbal communication.

1. **Visual communication** looks at your posture, body language, clothes and gestures. The first thing people notice

is your appearance. Make sure you're dressed appropriately for the occasion and that you're comfortable. Your posture should always be upright, and your body language should be open and energetic instead of closed-off and sluggish. Practise doing the Superman pose by placing your hands on your hips with your legs apart, and take deep breaths to feel secure and grounded before you speak.

2. **Vocal communication** involves your tone of voice and the pace at which you speak. The top speakers in the world are excellent storytellers. They know how to create anticipation, they know when to speed things up and slooooow them down so they can land their point. Most importantly, they speak with conviction. They speak as though they truly believe in every. single. word. they are saying.

My number one rule for public speaking is to only speak about things you really know and care about. Passion is important if you want to captivate your audience. Also, if you're giving a presentation or speaking in public, don't do the whole thing in one tone of voice. When you want to get your audience excited by an idea, speak more quickly with more energy. When you want people to feel the impact and weight of a point, then slow down with calmer energy.

Another thing: don't be afraid of the silence. Silence can be a powerful tool in helping your message sink in. It doesn't have to be awkward.

3. **Verbal communication** is about the content of what you're actually saying. If you want to be a confident communicator,

you need to know your stuff. Do your research, practise, and use language that your audience will understand and relate to. Fancy words don't make you look smarter. Let your message be accessible.

HOW TO CONFIDENTLY HAVE DIFFICULT CONVERSATIONS

It's one thing to be a confident communicator when everything is going according to plan, but what happens when things become a bit challenging?

Here are five steps you can take:

1. Have the conversation

Avoiding tough conversations in order not to upset people can cause you to harbour resentment and unforgiveness, which seriously outweighs the benefits of staying quiet and keeping the peace. Also, our meaning-making machine of a brain will start making assumptions, trying to 'mind-read' the situation, which makes things look worse than they actually are.

Apply everything you learned in Chapter 6 about overcoming fear and just do it!

2. Be open and listen

Once you've brought up the issue, be open and listen to what the other person has to say in response.

Don't just listen to respond with a script you've already created in your head. Really listen to understand their point of view and reasoning.

3. Use 'I' statements

The moment you start pointing fingers at someone, they'll get defensive. When their guard is up, communication shuts down, and nobody wins. Using statements like 'from my perspective …', 'I felt this way when you did this …', 'This is what I understood from what was said …' will keep the conversation focused on your experience, and not on judgements you've made about the other person.

4. Be solutions-orientated

Before you start a difficult conversation, have a few ideas for how the situation can be resolved or for positive changes that can be made, so the other person can see you are committed to finding a way forward and not instigating conflict for no reason.

5. Follow up after some time

Always check in a few days or weeks later with the person you've had the difficult conversation with. Sometimes people need a bit more time to process information, so following up and checking in makes sure the person knows that they matter and are heard.

And if you're on the receiving end of a difficult conversation, try not to internalize it by thinking someone is calling you a bad person. Be open and listen, take on the lessons you've learned, and commit to doing better next time.

CAN INTROVERTS BE CONFIDENT COMMUNICATORS?

Confident communication isn't just reserved for extroverts. Whether you're an introvert, an extrovert, or a bit of both, you can learn to communicate with confidence. Again, this isn't just about being the loudest in the room, it's about showing up with an energy that says:

- 'I know who I am.'
- 'I trust in my abilities.'
- 'I deserve to be here.'

Introverted readers, I'd love to encourage you to take the fundamentals of the 3 V's and apply them in your life in a way that works for you. Introversion isn't about a lack of confidence but actually just a characteristic of those who get energy from internal thought and solitude versus those who get energy from social interaction and attention (extroverts). In fact, many of us have both introvert and extrovert tendencies – it's rarely either/or.

The goal here is to understand your personality traits and use them to your advantage. For example, according to Susan Cain, author of *Quiet Power*, introverts tend to make amazing leaders and entrepreneurs because they are creative thinkers, good listeners, and not obsessed with power. In a negotiation, being a good listener means you can pick up on cues other people tend to miss. As an entrepreneur, it allows you to fully understand the needs of your customers so you can confidently create solutions to meet those needs. And in relationships, it allows your partner to know they are seen and heard, which builds trust and an environment for you to show up as your true, authentic self.

If you look at the ingredients of powerful communication – looking the part, speaking with authority, conviction, passion, knowing your stuff, and listening intently – they can all be accessed by both introverts and extroverts.

OWNING YOUR SUCCESS

In Chapter 8, I introduced the Monthly Wins Tracker (see also page 99) to help you acknowledge your successes, but from time to time, you've got to go one step further and actually *talk* about them. Yes, that's right, getting comfortable with self-promotion and openly talking about your successes is a vital part of building confidence and the third part of embracing your main character energy.

I know as soon as I said 'self-promotion', some of you already started feeling cringed out by the idea, but in all honesty, 'self-promotion' isn't a bad word. There's self-promotion that sounds like boasting, and there's self-promotion that helps you build credibility. We're going to learn how to do the latter.

Get strategic about showcasing your expertise and building a reputation, so the people looking for what you have can find you.

For me, self-promotion has always been an exchange of value and enthusiasm: you have something to offer the world (value), and someone out there needs what you have (enthusiasm). Instead of waiting for them to magically find you, you get strategic about showcasing your expertise, sharing your knowledge, and building a track record. By showing up consistently, you increase your visibility, you build connections, and increase your opportunities.

I know there is an argument for moving in silence, not sharing your dreams with everyone, and not letting your left hand know what your right hand is doing, because not everyone wants to see you win, and the haters are real. However, we can learn to be selective in what we share and how we share it, so we don't completely cancel out all the benefits of self-promotion.

MYTHS AND TRUTHS ABOUT SELF-PROMOTION

Here are some myths and truths about self-promotion to help you reframe it in a way that can be used to build your confidence:

Myth: It's arrogant, it's superficial, it makes you look full of yourself.

Truth: There's a difference between confidence and arrogance ...

Arrogant people only think of themselves. They want to be at the top and push everyone else below them. They have an 'I'm better than you' mentality, and they shout about their accomplishments in a very self-centred and boastful way.

Confident people, on the other hand, know that they are amazing, but they think about how they can use their gifts to lift others up. When confident people self-promote and talk about their accomplishments, they focus mostly on the lessons they've learned and how those lessons can be used to help and inspire other people.

Myth: Promoting yourself makes other people feel bad about themselves.

Truth: When you do it in the right way, people tend to be more inspired by your success than demoralized by it.

This is why aspirational marketing is so powerful. Behavioural scientists have also studied the power of role models in getting young people to follow a positive trajectory in life, and research shows that if people of a similar background to you see you win, it opens up their minds to believe it's also possible for them.[9] Because if you can do it, they can too.

If you celebrate yourself in an authentic and inclusive way and people still feel a certain way about it, you've got to make peace with the fact that, at the end of the day, you are not responsible for other people's emotions. If someone feels insecure about themselves after seeing you succeed, that's a choice they've made and they need to ask themselves why you winning is triggering them in a negative way. As I always say:

If my light is too bright for you, go and put some sunglasses on.

#CAKIMANTRA

9 Sanders, Michael, 'More Evidence on the Power of Role Models', *The Behavioural Insights Team* (31 July 2017). https://www.bi.team/blogs/more-evidence-on-the-power-of- role-models/

You're not here to please, you're here to live the one life you have to the fullest! If they don't like you or your energy, they can leave the room. But no more shrinking. You are the main character. Own it.

Research shows that if people of a similar background to you see you win, it opens up their minds to believe it's also possible for them.

Myth: I just need to put my head down and let my work do the talking.

Truth: Your work will not speak for itself alone.

Society has sold women the lie that we need to keep our heads down and let our work speak for itself, but data shows that 21 per cent of women are more likely to be passed over for promotion compared to their male counterparts, so something isn't adding up![10]

There is no award for being the world's best-kept secret.

#CAKIMANTRA

---

10 Bayern, Macy, 'Women Are 21% Less Likely To Be Promoted Than Male Coworkers', TechRepublic (28 November 2018). https://www.techrepublic.com/article/ women-are-21-less-likely-to-be-promoted-than-male- coworkers/

Hiding your gifts isn't the same thing as being humble. You can be humble and still believe you are good enough to succeed. You can be humble and celebrate yourself for how far you've come. A lot of people use being humble as an excuse not to own their accomplishments, but there are really a couple of things hiding behind that fake humility. One of them is imposter syndrome – you downplay your achievements because you're afraid that if people dig into your success, they'll find out that you're not that good and you don't really know what you're doing. When you play small, there's less risk of judgement and shame, so you stay in your comfort zone, saying you're humble when you're really just hiding from your greatness.

You downplay your achievements because you're afraid that if people dig into your success, they'll find out that you're not that good and you don't really know what you're doing.

Another thing that hides behind being humble is a fear of judgement; this one isn't actually that surprising as studies show that women who self-promote and speak authoritatively sometimes experience backlash for failing to show stereotypical 'feminine traits' (such as being humble, nurturing and collaborative).[11]

---

11 Phelan, Julie E. et al., 'Competent Yet Out in the Cold: Shifting Criteria for Hiring Reflect Backlash Toward Agentic Women', *Psychology of Women Quarterly*, 32 (2008). DOI:10.1111/j.1471-6402.2008.00454.x; Rudman, Laurie A. and Peter Glick 'Prescriptive Gender Stereotypes and Backlash Toward Agentic Women', *Journal of Social Issues*, 57 (2002). DOI: 10.1111/0022- 4537.00239.

It's a double-edged sword: engage in self-promotion and run the risk of being criticized for being boastful or arrogant, or fail to self-promote and limit your growth by getting sidelined and not taken seriously.

Can we ever win? I like to believe we can. Is the backlash fair? No. But we can't wait for gender bias to be eliminated before we live life to the fullest.

So, what can we do? Focus on what we can control and use the resources available to us. The tools I've shared in this chapter can help you work around the hurdles you might encounter as a woman who is confident and unapologetic in owning her accomplishments. Here are a few more ideas to consider:

- Host a 'Lunch & Learn' session at work to showcase your knowledge, skills, passion and accomplishments in a certain area.
- Create a culture or habit of celebration by starting or ending meetings or gatherings with each individual sharing a recent win – I personally do this with my team.
- Put together a report of best practices, lessons learned and team accomplishments after you've wrapped up a project and cascade it to senior management, clients or share as a case study.
- Be a cheerleader for others and encourage them to celebrate their wins when you see them happen.

On the whole, sharing your success alongside the lessons you've learned and best practices for others to implement ensures you're lifting others as you climb. If you still get labelled as arrogant or aggressive when you're unapologetic in communicating your value and speaking up for yourself, escalate the situation to HR for further support, and consider whether the environment is worth staying in. Protect your sanity and choose your battles.

OWNING YOUR PERSONAL STORY

Every main character has a storyline. If you want to step fully into your main character energy, you need to create and own your story.

Humans connect through stories. We trust, buy from, and give opportunities to people we feel emotionally connected to. That's where your personal brand comes in – it's the bridge between who you are and the impact you want to make.

A strong personal brand isn't just for entrepreneurs and influencers. Freelancers who ignore their digital presence risk losing business, and professionals on the career ladder risk being overlooked. Whether online or at work, your reputation is your currency. Build trust, deliver value, and people will champion you, recommend you, and open doors you didn't even know existed.

Everyone already has a reputation. Building a personal brand is simply choosing to own your narrative, instead of letting others write it for you.

When you tell a powerful story, people share it. Owning your story multiplies your impact, amplifies your main character energy, and inspires others to step into theirs too.

Everyone already has a reputation. Building a personal brand is simply choosing to own your narrative, instead of letting others write it for you.

BUILD YOUR PERSONAL BRAND

Instead of letting the world put labels on you, take charge. Here are three steps to build a personal brand that feels authentic, organic and trustworthy.

STEP 1:
IDENTIFY YOUR USP
Ask yourself:

1. What problem do I see (or solve) that fires me up? For me, it was the generational cycle of low self-esteem in women and girls.
2. What do I want to be known for? Which traits should people associate with me? *(Tip: align this with your Power Circle – strengths, passions, values.)*
3. What projects have I worked on, and how did my input make them successful?
4. What projects or tasks do people naturally trust me with?
5. Which industries, roles or communities do I actually want to be part of?

Look for patterns in your answers and get intentional about building on them.

Quick caveat: We live in the era of multi-hyphenates, so you don't need to be known for just one thing. The goal is to build a universe. Start with a core theme, then expand into complementary areas. While it's OK to be multi-passionate, don't dilute your brand with random, disconnected interests.

STEP 2:
COMMUNICATE YOUR USP

Once you know your themes, share them. Your personal brand comes alive through connection – online (social, email, content) and offline (networking, conversations, workshops). Use your voice, style and story to let people in. Here are four content and conversation prompts to help you speak about yourself and your brand in a way that connects with people and feels authentic to you:

1. **Your Stand**: Talk about things that matter to you; where do you stand on industry challenges and social controversies?
2. **Your Life Stories**: Talk about your journey, your wins and losses, your strengths and weaknesses, behind the scenes in your life.
3. **Thought Leadership**: Talk about interesting articles or facts you've read recently. Share your perspective, showcase your knowledge.
4. **Your Results**: Talk about the impact your work is having and the lessons you've learned along the way, share case studies, good reviews and accolades.

STEP 3:
CHOOSE CHANNELS AND STAY CONSISTENT

If you're new to this and starting from scratch, don't burn out trying to be everywhere, all at the same time. Pick a core platform that is widely used by your target audience and fits your communication style:

- **For visual storytellers/conversationalists:** Instagram, TikTok, YouTube, Pinterest.
- **For writers/deep thinkers:** LinkedIn, Substack, X, Reddit, Threads.

Consistency matters more than presence everywhere. Repurpose content, plan ahead, and keep showing up.

FINAL WORD

Building a personal brand takes effort, but it's worth it. Every main character knows their worth, owns their story, and communicates it with confidence. Celebrate your wins. Be your own cheerleader. Because your opinion of yourself matters more than what other people think of you.

As we learned in the PERMA model for optimum wellness (see also page 7), research from positive psychologists shows that people who look back on their life with a sense of accomplishment feel more optimistic and confident about their future. Celebrating yourself by owning your successes isn't arrogant – it's an essential pillar of your well-being.

Learn to fall in love with your story and embrace the fact that no matter how big or small your achievements, you are always worthy of sharing your voice and celebrating your success.

Every main character knows their worth, owns their story, and communicates it with confidence.

In the next chapter, we'll continue building on main character energy by learning how to prioritize our needs.

10

PRIORITIZING YOUR NEEDS

Every time you're given a choice between disappointing someone else and disappointing yourself, your duty is to disappoint that someone else. Your job throughout your entire life is to disappoint as many people as it takes to avoid disappointing yourself.

– GLENNON DOYLE

As we wrap up this journey, it's time to talk about creating *long-term* well-being instead of the yo-yo self-care cycle so many of us live in – work hard, burn out, crash out, rest, repeat. Life doesn't have to be that way. A fancy holiday won't fix structural problems. True success is being confident, wealthy *and* well rested (I really like the sound of that: #WealthyAndWellRested).

Would you really do all the work of building a growth mindset, overcoming fear, and embracing your main character energy, only to throw it away because people don't like that you're finally prioritizing yourself? Absolutely not.

The writer and activist Glennon Doyle said it best: nobody dies from being disappointed. If you have to set boundaries, choose yourself and put your health first. Because if you burn out, who's going to do the work anyway?

Burnout is more than being tired. It's a total loss of energy, interest, and ability to function after chronic overwork. It often shows up as:

- **Emotional exhaustion:** Wild mood swings, constant irritation, or feeling completely numb.
- **Mental overload:** Everyday tasks feel impossible, decisions paralyse you, and joy disappears.
- **Neglect of self:** Skipped meals, no rest, endless work, and disconnect from your body.
- **Physical strain:** Headaches, body aches, insomnia, anxiety, even tightness in your chest.

If this feels familiar, it's your body's way of saying: enough is enough.

DITCHING THE PEOPLE-PLEASER IN YOU

One of the reasons I burned out was the people-pleaser in me. I was a full-on *yes* person, classic Superwoman syndrome. I tied my worth to how much I could do for others, and it nearly broke me.

Society trains us to think saying 'no' makes us selfish, while saying 'yes' makes us reliable and worthy. Of course, we all want to feel needed, but not at the expense of our health. The key word here is *balance*.

It is possible to please others without neglecting your own physical and emotional needs.

#CAKIMANTRA

Prioritizing yourself isn't selfish. It's strategic. Fill your cup first, then give from the overflow. Nobody wins when you're burned out and running on empty.

If you take on more than you can handle, you are also literally opening the door to imposter syndrome. But you're not suffering from it because you're incapable of doing your job; rather it's that you've overstretched yourself and the expectations on yourself were unrealistic.

Before you can quit people-pleasing, you've got to be aware of how it shows up in your life.

You're a people-pleaser if:

- You find it hard to say 'no' and end up doing things you don't want to.
- You prioritize others' needs while ignoring your own.
- You avoid conflict at all costs.
- You apologize too much – even when it isn't needed.
- You dim your voice or light to make others comfortable.
- You often feel resentful because you give more than you get.

If these sound familiar, don't panic! Being a people-pleaser comes from a very natural human desire to be loved and accepted. The issue arises when we go the extra mile for other people and do the bare minimum for ourselves. Stop under-valuing yourself – you are worthy of the same love and attention you give others.

THE DANGER OF ALWAYS SAYING 'YES'

Being 'too nice' often attracts the wrong people. People who tend to neglect themselves in order to please others often attract users. I hate to break it to you, but they're not always asking you for help because they like you or you're the best person for the job – they're asking you because you're the person most likely to say 'yes'.

So, before you agree, pause and ask yourself:

- If I say 'yes' to this, what am I saying 'no' to in my own life?
- Am I doing this because I *want* to, or because I feel pressured?
- Do I really have capacity, or am I afraid of disappointing someone?
- How do I feel after spending time with this person?

If you keep saying 'yes' to everyone and everything while saying 'no' to yourself and your dreams, you will burn out, and I can tell you, burnout ain't cute! Let's learn how to work smart and rest well.

HOW TO REST WITHOUT FEELING GUILTY

Rest isn't a 'nice to have'. It's not a luxury reward you get from overworking yourself. Rest is essential.

#CAKIMANTRA

No one has ever said, 'I'll eat once I've achieved my goals,' because food is essential fuel for the body, and you most likely won't achieve anything on an empty stomach. I want you to prioritize rest the same way and refuel your body, mind and soul so you can achieve long-lasting wellness.

Rest isn't just sleep or Netflix binges. According to Dr Saundra Dalton-Smith, author of *Sacred Rest*, we need different types of rest: physical, mental, emotional, social and spiritual. Pay attention to which one you need most right now. To avoid or bounce back from burnout, make sure you're resting in the way that your body, mind and soul need at that moment.

PHYSICAL REST	
WHEN YOU NEED IT	**HOW TO DO IT**
When you feel exhausted, can't keep your eyes open or feel really stiff with body pains.	Get more sleep. Get a massage or a hot bath. Stretch your body, do some yoga or gentle exercise. Moisturize your skin, then use a dry brush to get your blood flowing. Eat a healthy and wholesome meal.

EMOTIONAL REST	
WHEN YOU NEED IT	**HOW TO DO IT**
When your heart feels heavy, your emotions swing or feel numb and you're easily irritated or consistently low.	Do something fun to spark joy and prioritize what really matters to you. Process and release your emotions with the 3 A's on page 32. Practise gratitude and reflect on your monthly wins. Tidy and refresh your space, a clean room = a clean mind.

SOCIAL REST	
WHEN YOU NEED IT	**HOW TO DO IT**
When your social batteries are drained and you dread seeing people or when you're feeling low, disconnected and craving a supportive community.	**Social rest with people:** Share a meal. Spa days. Video calls. **Social rest from people:** Solo trips/dates. Long nature walks. Time offline.

MENTAL REST	
WHEN YOU NEED IT	**HOW TO DO IT**
When your brain feels foggy, you're struggling to concentrate, you're lacking creativity and you're heavy on the selfcriticism.	Less time online, more offline. Meditating and journalling. Learn something new in a book or podcast. Change of scenery.

SPIRITUAL REST	
WHEN YOU NEED IT	**HOW TO DO IT**
When you feel there's something missing in life or you've lost your sense of direction, purpose and inner wisdom.	Do something meaningful to help others, like volunteering. Put a smile on their face. Meditate and pray. Reconnect with your faith and listen to an inspiring message of hope. Make a vision board.

FINANCIAL REST	
WHEN YOU NEED IT	**HOW TO DO IT**
When money stress, debt worries or poor spending habits leave you anxious or ashamed.	Challenge negative beliefs and replace shame with honest reflection.. Pause compulsive spending with a 48-hour rule. Create saving pots for lifestyle and enjoyment. Connect money goals to your values, and shift from short-term decisions to long-term financial planning that prioritizes your future self.

P.S These are my personal tips for better financial wellness and should not be taken as legal financial advice.

A ROUTINE THAT WORKS

One of my favourite wellness routines comes from Jay Shetty's book *Think Like a Monk*. His T.I.M.E. model is a simple way to centre yourself before the world starts demanding things from you:

- **T – Thankfulness:** Write, say, or share one thing you're grateful for. Gratitude rewires your brain for joy.
- **I – Insight:** Learn something new – a book, podcast, or TED Talk. Growth fuels confidence.
- **M – Meditation:** Ten to fifteen minutes of stillness. Try breathwork, visualizations, or affirmations.
- **E – Exercise:** Move your body. Release stress and boost energy.

Even ten minutes in each area sets you up to win the day.

STOP FEELING GUILTY ABOUT REST

Knowing how to rest is easy. Giving yourself *permission* to rest is the real work.

Here are reminders for guilt-free rest:

- Rest is not laziness. It's fuel.
- Self-care is not selfish. It's survival.
- Productivity isn't the measure of your worth.
- You don't need to earn rest – you already deserve it.

On busy days, when rest is the last thing on your mind remember:

- You're most productive when you're energized, not drained.
- Don't wait to 'find' time – *create* it. Put it in your diary.

- Wellness supports your goals. It's not a distraction from them.

Self-care is a necessity. You need it, you deserve it, and you don't have to earn it through hard work.

At the end of the day, learning to prioritize your needs is a mindset shift. If you feel guilty about rest, take a moment to redefine what rest means to you and look at how it can help you move forward in life. Self-care is a necessity. You need it, you deserve it, and you don't have to earn it through hard work.

Rest Affirmations

Repeat these often, out loud or in your journal, to reprogram your mind:

- I deserve joy and fulfilment, even in hard seasons.
- My worth is not tied to pleasing others.
- When I pour into myself, I shine brighter for others.
- I am worthy of having my needs met.
- Rest is always an investment, never a waste of time.

SETTING BOUNDARIES AND PROTECTING YOUR ENERGY

Once you've broken through the guilt of prioritizing yourself, the next step is setting boundaries. Boundaries are simply your *user manual*, showing people who you are, what you value, and how you want to be treated.

What You Gain From Boundaries

Every boundary is a 'yes' to yourself:

- 'Yes' to having your needs met. 'No' to feeling anger and resentment.
- 'Yes' to peace and safety. 'No' to feeling disrespected and unsettled by certain people and places.
- 'Yes' to energy and joy. 'No' to things that drain you.
- 'Yes' to confidence and self-worth. 'No' to anxiety, stress, and feeling unworthy.
- 'Yes' to attracting the right people and letting go of the wrong ones.

So, in short: boundaries = freedom.

Communicate With Confidence

Many women fear being 'aggressive' when they simply need to be assertive. Remember the difference: aggression disregards others; assertiveness honours both sides. Setting boundaries does not mean being harsh and cutting people off. You can communicate your needs with compassion and grace.

THE PASSIVE PERSON	THE AGGRESSIVE PERSON	THE ASSERTIVE PERSON
Afraid to speak up or speaks very quietly.	Interrupts and talks over others.	Speaks openly, knows when to talk and when to listen.
Values others above themselves; neglects personal needs.	Values themselves above others and disregards impact.	Sees themselves as equal to others; balances needs and compromise.
Avoids conflict, even against their own values.	Creates conflict through selfish demands.	Doesn't instigate conflict but remains confident and keeps integrity.

Examples of compassionate assertiveness:

- 'I'm not in a good place to support right now. Can we talk later?'
- 'I can't lend money, but here's another way I could help.'
- 'Things are busy; I need some me-time. I'll check in when I'm recharged.'

Never be afraid of losing people by speaking your truth or stating your needs. It's your responsibility to tell them where your boundaries are, and if people stop being there for you because you've started prioritizing your needs, then they never really cared for you in the first place.

When you don't settle for the bare minimum, you make room for bigger and better opportunities to come.

#CAKIMANTRA

Setting Boundaries At Work

Work is part of life, not all of it. Setting professional boundaries is crucial. Situations where you'll need to assert yourself include:

- Colleagues taking credit for your ideas.
- Being asked to work unreasonable hours.
- Unnecessary meetings draining your time.
- Messages outside work hours.
- Guilt-tripping over taking time off.

Although it can be more daunting because of the power dynamics, setting boundaries at work is similar to setting boundaries in your personal life: understand and articulate what the problem is, know your non-negotiables, know what your preferred outcome is, and then confidently communicate those desires.

For example:

- 'I'd appreciate being credited when you share my ideas. Can you do that going forward?'
- 'To do my best work, I can't take on extra tasks right now. Let's revisit when my workload is lighter.'
- 'Please schedule emails during office hours – I'll respond promptly then.'

Skip the apologetic fluff, like 'Sorry to bother you' or 'No worries if not'. Boundaries aren't rude – they make sure everyone is on the same page.

If you find that your boundaries are repeatedly disregarded, you might be working in the wrong environment and it's time to find somewhere that respects your personal and professional needs.

WRAPPING UP

I want you to make a promise to yourself that from here on out, you will regard yourself as highly as you regard those around you and prioritize your own needs.

As you go through life, discovering your authentic self, getting sassy with the Mean Girl, taking risks, embracing your main character energy and celebrating your success, remember none of this would be possible without a well-rested body, mind and soul.

Prioritize yourself. Set boundaries. Make peace with the fact that you will outgrow some people and places. That's OK. When one door closes, another opens.

There is no one else like you in the world. You deserve to be taken care of, pampered and loved. By yourself as well as by others.

You are a priority. Never forget that.

CONCLUSION

At the beginning of this book, I asked if you had ever thought of what it would be like to have unshakeable confidence. Whatever your answer was, I hope it feels a lot more achievable for you by this point. As we come to the end of this journey, my wish is that you are filled with hope. Not merely wishful thinking, but real hope that leads to determination, drive, and a desire to give yourself the best possible life you can imagine. I know you are worthy of that – and now you do too. That's the best part.

So, what's next?

I can't promise that after reading this you'll never doubt yourself ever again, because you will. Confidence isn't the absence of self-doubt. It's about noticing the fear, the doubt, and the imposter syndrome as signals that you must take action.

Your greatest insecurities are often directly tied to your greatest strengths, so when you feel that you don't deserve to be heard, speaking up is exactly what you must do.

When you feel you're not worthy of an opportunity, go for it! Pursuing it despite your insecurities is exactly what you must do.

When you feel you don't deserve rest, rest is exactly what you owe yourself.

Before reading this book, you may have been hiding your light, you may have been at the mercy of your Mean Girl, or you may have been crippled by your past failures and rejections. From this point on, these things no longer have power over you. You're not the same person you were when you started this book. You're awake now. And the awakened version of you has to start making better choices and creating new habits for the long run. Confidence is a practice, so if you think the job is done once you put down this book, well, think again. It's a never-ending journey and thankfully, you'll always have this book of practical tools and proven strategies to guide you through future challenges.

When you feel you're not worthy of an opportunity, go for it! Pursuing it despite your insecurities is exactly what you must do.

At its core, this book equips you to thrive and flourish no matter what life throws at you. You now have the tools to identify and articulate your strengths, passions, values and purpose, which will make sure you are living a fulfilled life in alignment with your calling.

Confidence isn't a destination you arrive at overnight, so if you're still processing and need more time to deal with feelings that have come up for you, take that time – and ask for help when you need it. It will be worth it. You now have the tools, mindset and confidence to go forth and kill it. Get excited by the fact that every baby step is bringing you closer to your truest, most powerful self.

And if one day you wake up and realize the things you value and desire have changed, that's OK too. It's a sign of growth – and an opportunity for you to start this beautiful journey again, heading in a better direction. You can set out many times, learning and loving yourself over and over again until your very last days.

At the end of every coaching call, I give my clients the opportunity to make some commitments to themselves – promises from this new place of enlightenment that they will honour. I want you to do the same.

What promises are you going to make to yourself today?

Confidence is about keeping the promises you make to yourself, so when you write these promises, write them with conviction. Know why they are important to you and follow through on them. Don't make promises you think I'd want to see, or promises you think will impress the world – these promises are for you.

And if you don't always manage to keep them, just give yourself the compassion you so readily give to others and make sure you get back up again.

What you believe about yourself is the foundation of everything you do. Your opinion of yourself matters more than what anyone else thinks, so never let anyone else place limitations on your life. It's better to be full of yourself than be full of other people's negative opinions that, frankly, do not matter! You are skilled, you have strengths, and your potential is limitless!

And one of the beautiful things about being confident is that it's not something we have to compete for. There's enough room for all of us to be confident and thrive. So, share the wisdom you've gained from this book. Buy a copy for a woman or girl in your life. The next time you're in a room and it feels like the insecurity Olympics, be the person who changes the narrative, because no one wins when we are stuck in a vicious cycle of self-hate. Most importantly, be the change you want to see in the world.

I'd love you to share your Confident and Killing It moments (#CAKIMoments) with me online and keep tracking your wins in your Monthly Wins Tracker to remind yourself you are absolutely good enough and to inspire other women who see you 'Killing it' to believe they can do the same. If you're like me and love to write and reflect as you read, I've created an interactive digital workbook linked at the back to guide you through the exercises in this book and help you deepen your learnings.

And if you're more of a visual learner, check out my online course at confidentandkillingit.com or scan the QR code at the back. The course is where I break down the key concepts from this book step by step and help you build your very own personal game plan for confidence.

Because reading is just the start. True transformation comes when you *apply* what you've learned.

Finally, life's way more fun when we're all Confident and Killing It *together*, so don't do this journey alone. Join our incredible community of ambitious women and stay connected with us via socials and the newsletter. Although this is the end of this book, it's the beginning of an exciting new chapter for us all.

Beyond the Book with
Tiwalola Adebayo of *Confident & Killing It*

Scan this QR code for an interactive digital workbook and my online course where I break down the key concepts of the book to help you build your own personalised confidence game plan.

INDEX

Note: page numbers in **bold** refer to diagrams.